Living With a Listed Building

The Essential Guide to
owning, maintaining,
repairing and improving
your historic property.

Josephine M Cormier. ARIBA

Published by:

Courtland Books,
28 Wytham Street,
Oxford,
OX1 4TS

Tel: 01865 244168

ISBN 0-0952553-1-7

Whilst every care has been taken in the preparation
of the information contained in this book, no liabil-
ity can be accepted for any loss or damage arising
either directly or indirectly out of reliance on this
book or any part of it. This book contains general
advice only and in specific cases specialised legal or
technical advice should be sought.

Thanks

The Author would like to thank Jane Eastman, E.T.I Eyston and Rita
Morey for their help in the preparation of this book.

Front Cover and Chapter Illustrations by Lance Golding - 01635-34414
Desk Top Publishing by Grafx Resource - 01635-45804

Introduction

We live in surroundings which combine both old and new buildings. The old buildings are special. By giving us a link with the past, they enrich our lives and provide an established background for life today.

Buildings, like people, need care and attention in order to survive. Old buildings, like old people, need more care and attention and because of their age, they are less able to adapt to change and are more likely to give way under the pressures of time.

In an effort to strike a balance between old and new, some buildings are listed as being of Special Architectural or Historic Interest and laws have been made to protect them.

Owning a Listed Building is both a privilege and a burden, for whilst owners have something considered to be of national importance, they are expected to keep their property in repair and to preserve its character.

Buildings have always been changed for the convenience of their users, with the result that fewer and fewer old features survive.

For the owners of Listed Buildings, it may sometimes seem as though everyone is against them, trying to stop them doing what past owners have done. What has happened is a change in priorities. Now the law asks us to think a little more about the building as a special entity and a little less about our own comfort and convenience.

This book has been written to encourage owners to understand and enjoy their Listed Buildings. To help them overcome some of the problems and misunderstandings which they may come across in dealing with the law and in trying to keep their building in good repair.

Contents

Chapter Three - How Do I Apply for Listed Building Consent?

Chapter Four - Appealing against a Refusal, or Conditions

Chapter Five - Dereliction, Grants and VAT

Chapter Six - Living with a Listed Building

Chapter Seven - The Roof

Chapter Eight - Rainwater, Drainage and Damp

Chapter Nine - The Walls

Chapter Ten - Doors, Windows and Fireplaces

General Conclusions
Glossary
Extract from Archaeological Survey
Model Application Form & Plans
Useful Addresses

Chapter One

The Basic Questions

Chapter One
The Basic Questions

What is a Listed Building?

A Listed Building is a building included in the Statutory List of Buildings of Special Architectural or Historic Interest. This list is drawn up by the Secretary of State for National Heritage in England and the Secretary of State for Wales in Wales.

In England the actual production of the Lists is done by staff of "English Heritage" (The Historic Buildings and Monuments' Commission for England). In Wales it is done by staff of the Welsh Office.

Scotland has its own legislation, which is similar.

Why are buildings listed?

The surroundings in which we live have a profound effect on the quality of our lives. Buildings and the spaces between and around them go to make up those surroundings.

Old buildings are visible links with the past which provide a background for present day life. Grouped together they form our towns and villages. They can easily be lost by demolition or alteration. 'Listing' buildings is a way of identifying those which are important reminders of past traditions and a way of protecting them for the enjoyment of future generations. People have always altered or demolished buildings in the past, but during this century, the rate of alteration and demolition has increased. Concern about the loss of older buildings, resulted in the 1947 Town and Country Planning Act being passed which included powers to control alteration and demolition of some of these buildings.

The Lists were made to identify the buildings worth protecting and as a guide to local authorities when dealing with this Act. Over the years the law relating to Listed Buildings was expanded and refined resulting at present in the "Planning (Listed Buildings and Conservation Areas) Act 1990".

How are the buildings chosen?

The name of the List tells you something about this. The buildings are "special" and they may have either "architectural" or "historic" interest, or both. Age, rarity and condition are all relevant.

"Architectural Interest" - This does not necessarily mean that the building is the work of a particular architect, but that it has some "special" interest as a building.

The following guidelines are used:-

A. Buildings built before 1700 which survive in anything like their original condition will be included.

B. Most buildings from 1700 to 1840 are included but there is some selection. For example if a building of this period is very much altered it will not be included.

C. Buildings from 1840 to 1914 need to have some particular quality and character. In this group the works of principal architects come into play.

D. Buildings from 1914 to 1939 must be of a very high quality to be included.

"Historic Interest" - This is less well defined, but generally buildings associated with well known characters or events, particular examples of social and economic history (e.g. railway stations), or technological innovations (e.g. early use of concrete) will be included.

It is not just buildings which can be occupied which are listed. Structures such as garden walls, railings, gates, statues, grottoes, milestones, tombs, gravestones, bridges, etc. can all be listed individually. So you could own a house with garden walls, railings and gates at the front, a statue in the garden and a milestone on the road outside, all of which can be separately listed.

Who does the actual choosing and when is it done?

At first, staff of the Department of the Environment drew up the lists. This went along quite slowly for few people were employed on this, and there was the whole country to cover.

During the late 1970s, in England, it was decided to speed up the process and extra Inspectors were employed. Some of the work was also farmed out to the staff of County Councils, Local Authorities and specialists from the private sector in the attempt to cover the ground as quickly as possible.

That "re-survey" is now complete and it is unlikely that such a comprehensive exercise will be carried out again. Theoretically every building in the country has been assessed, but because of the speed of the work and new information coming to light, there are bound to be some buildings which have been missed or mistakes made. This possibility is covered in the Act. Buildings are continually being added to the List through the work of local authorities, amenity societies and individuals who draw attention to buildings which, for whatever reason have been overlooked.

Can a building be listed quickly?

If a Local Authority considers that an unlisted building is of special architectural or historic interest and it is in danger of being demolished or altered so as to affect its character, then the authority can serve a "Building Preservation Notice" on the owner and occupier of the building.

This effectively lists the building for a period of six months during which time the Secretary of State must decide whether or not to include the building on the main list.

If the Secretary of State decides not to list the building, then no further notice can be served for another twelve months. The owner can then ask the Local Authority for compensation if he feels he has suffered loss or damage.

How do I find out if my building is Listed?

If your building was listed when you bought it, this should have shown up in the searches made with the Local Authority by your solicitor.

If your building has been listed since you bought it, then you should have received a letter from the Local Authority informing you and giving you some information about what it means.

If neither of these has happened or you would like to see a copy of the actual lists they are available for public inspection and are kept by English Heritage, County Councils and District Councils. Each Authority has its own way of doing this. Sometimes the lists are kept in the main libraries, sometimes at the County Record Office.

The most likely place to find a copy is at your Local Council Planning Department. If you are not sure which Local Council, it is the Authority to which the Council Tax for that building is paid.

What does a List look like?

The latest Lists are in book form and have green covers with the Royal Arms at the top and the name of the District, County, and Parishes covered at the bottom. They are divided into Parishes.

Inside, the first page gives the date of issue at the top. Make a note of this, for future reference. The second page explains how the entries are set out. The third page tells you how many buildings in each grade are listed. After that, comes the list set out in the following form for each building.

Here is an example:-

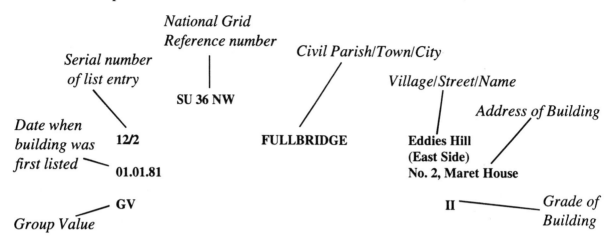

Serial number of list entry

National Grid Reference number

Civil Parish/Town/City

Village/Street/Name

Address of Building

Date when building was first listed

SU 36 NW

12/2

01.01.81

FULLBRIDGE

Eddies Hill (East Side)
No. 2, Maret House

GV

Group Value

II

Grade of Building

> House. Late C18. Slate roof with flanking chimneys. Brick walls, flemish bond, ground floor painted. Square plan. 2 storeys. 2 vertical sliding sash windows in reveals, dentil course at eaves, band at first floor, plinth. Central, six panelled door under plain, gabled hood on cut brackets. Interior, simple late C18 panelling to ground floor room on left of hall, straight flight stair with turned balusters. Forms a group with Nos. 1, 3 and 4 Eddies Hill.

Descriptive Notes

Date when first listed.

If there is no date given this is because it is beng included for the first time.

What does "Grade" mean?

There are two Grades:-

I   Buildings of exceptional interest, a small percentage of the total, e.g. Windsor Castle.

II   The majority of buildings - "of special interest". This grade has a sub grade II*, which is applied to buildings with some extra merit, for example a fine interior, which are not quite good enough to be rated I.In the past there was a third grade III, indicating buildings of local interest. These relate to older lists which have now been superseded. If the list shown to you includes this grade, ask whether there are any more recent lists available. Some libraries and record offices keep all past lists and staff do not always know the difference between them.

What does "Group Value" mean?

This is shown by the letters GV which mean that the building along with some of its neighbours forms an interesting group. It may even be part of a consciously designed set of buildings like The Crescent at Bath.

What do the descriptive notes mean?

The descriptive notes are not meant to cover every part of the building. They are done so that the building can be identified more easily on its site.

They have no legal significance and should not be treated as an exclusive record of all the features which make the building worthy of listing. This description is produced to a strict format, which is as follows:-

Building Type   e.g. "House"

Date   e.g. "Late C18" (C stands for Century) The dates can only be approximate for the Inspectors do not have time to do a comprehensive survey.

Architect   This only applies to buildings where the name of the architect is known.

Materials   Working down from the roof to the ground.

Plan   Overall shape of the building.

Facade   Number of storeys, then enough information about the main face of the building to identify it, for example: "Two windows" in this instance means two on each floor. Sometimes a building is described as having a number of "bays". This does not relate to windows. A "bay" is a vertical division of the building's structure.

Interior   Not always included, because Inspectors are not always able to go into each building. Again only the more obviously important features which have been seen by the Inspector will be included. Things which the Inspector did not see will not be included. This does not mean that they are not important.

Subsidiary Features   e.g. gates, urns etc. Not always included.

History   Not always included, but, if the building has historic significance, if for example "Jane Austen lived here", then this is where it would be noted.

Extra Information   e.g. whether the building has group value.

Sources   Not always included, but here would be noted any written sources of the building's history which the Inspector has had time to consult e.g. the Victoria County Histories (VCH).

Are only the things mentioned in the description Listed?

No. The whole building is covered by the legislation, inside and outside, back and side facades as well as everything attached to the building and within the "curtilage". This means that such things as garden walls and statues as well as separate buildings, like garden sheds, are covered, but only if built before 1948.

What is the curtilage?

This is an important and much debated question. There is, at present, no precise legal definition of "curtilage". The Concise Oxford Dictionary defines it as an "area attached to a dwelling house".

Usually the garden of a house is well defined and this would be taken to be the "curtilage". The problem comes when dealing with other types of building or with houses which have been divided or have had their original gardens sold off.

If you are in doubt about this, ask the Conservation Officer or the Area Planning Officer at your Local Planning Authority. (Government advice on this issue is provided in Planning Policy Guidance Note 15, issued by the Department of the Environment).

Can Buildings be taken off the List?

Yes, but there has to be some good reason why the building is no longer "special". Such a reason could come from a simple clerical error in the address on the List. e.g. the address given and the description of the building do not tie up. In some cases there was a lapse between survey and issue of the list and buildings were demolished or completely altered during that time.

If you think your building should not be included you can ask the Listing Section of the Department of the Environment to look at it again. To help them with this you should send photographs and a location plan with your letter.

Can Buildings be protected against being listed?

If Planning Permission has been applied for or given for alteration, extension or demolition of a building, the Act allows for a person to ask the Secretary of State for a certificate to say that he does not intend to List the building. This lasts for five years and during that time the Local Authority cannot serve a Building Preservation Notice. This is rarely used.

Chapter Two

The Scope
of the Controls

Chapter Two
The Scope of the Controls

Legal Background

Owning a Listed Building carries with it serious legal responsibilities.

The particular legislation which deals with Listed Buildings is "The Planning (Listed Buildings and Conservation Areas) Act 1990". This covers England and Wales, but not Scotland. This Act concerns both the drawing up of the Lists, mentioned in Chapter 1, and what can and cannot be done legally to a "Listed" Building.

Chapter 2 of this Act puts a restriction on works "affecting" Listed Buildings by making it a criminal offence to do works which "affect the character" of the building or to demolish a Listed Building without having got consent.

The Secretary of State for the National Heritage is responsible for drawing up the Lists and the Secretary of State for the Environment is responsible for Listed Building Consents.

Government Guidance

As well as the Act, the Government provides further advice and guidance in the form of Planning Policy Guidance Note 15 entitled "Planning and The Historic Environment".

This gives some idea of the thinking behind the legislation. It is aimed both at the Local Authorities and the public. It is available from the Department of the Environment and HMSO Books.

What is Listed Building Consent?

Listed Building Consent is the permission of the Local Planning Authority (or in some cases the Secretary of State) to do particular works to a listed building. Application is made on forms supplied by the Local Planning Authority and accompanied by appropriate drawings and specifications (see page 12).

Where do I go to get consent?

The Act is administered by Local Councils in most cases, but the Secretary of State for the Environment is responsible for deciding special cases and appeals against refusals.

What things do I need to get consent for?

- Demolition of all or any part of the building, or anything within the curtilage built before 1948.

- Any alteration or additions which "affect the character of the building". This covers the inside as well as the outside. Anything which is not strictly a repair to the existing fabric using matching materials is **LIKELY** to require consent.

Deciding on what needs consent can sometimes be difficult. Some things are obvious e.g. taking down a wall, altering windows, adding an extension, but smaller things, like replacing a guttering, or changing internal doors will also need consent. The question you must ask yourself is "Does this affect the character of the building?". In all cases you should obtain written confirmation from the Local Authority that consent is not required.

Is advice available from the Local Authority?

Many Councils employ specially trained staff called Conservation Officers to deal with Listed Buildings and they can help with specialised advice and local knowledge.

IT IS ESSENTIAL THAT YOU CHECK FIRST WITH YOUR LOCAL COUNCIL BEFORE DOING ANY WORK EVEN IF WHAT IS PROPOSED IS A REPAIR OR SEEMS TO BE INSIGNIFICANT.

Theoretically works of repair do not need consent, but opinions on what is repair and what is replacement differ and it is best to check before doing the work and get confirmation in writing.

What happens if I do work without getting consent?

This depends on what the work is. If it "affects the character" of the building, then you have committed criminal offence under the Act mentioned above, i.e. you have broken the law. This also applies if you do not carry out a condition put on a Listed Building Consent. (See Page 16).

If the work would have been given Listed Building Consent had that been applied for, then the staff of the Local Council may advise you to apply for retrospective consent. If asked, they may tell you how the work could be changed to become acceptable. It is always a good idea to ask for help.

What are the penalties for doing work without consent?

The Act covers anyone who does work without consent. That can be the owner, the builder and the architect. If you are found guilty in a magistrates' court, you can be sentenced to up to six months imprisonment, and/or a fine not exceeding £20,000.

If you are found guilty in a crown court, the penalties are up to two years imprisonment, and/or an unlimited fine. The court may set the fines to take account of any financial benefit you may make from the illegal works.

What else can happen when work is done without consent? (Listed Building Enforcement Notice).

Where the Local Planning Authority thinks that work is being or has been done without consent then a notice, called a "Listed Building Enforcement Notice" can be served. This is served on the owner, occupier and anyone else with an interest in the building e.g. a builder working on the site.

The notice must describe the work which has been done without consent, and what works must be done to restore the building to its former state. If this is not possible, it must outline what can be done to minimise the damage caused. If Listed Building Consent had been given but not complied with then the notice must say what works need to be done to comply.

There are penalties of imprisonment and fines like those mentioned earlier for not complying with a Listed Building Enforcement Notice. If a person is convicted and does not comply, then there is also a fine for every day after that conviction until the works required by the notice are put in hand.

Can I appeal against an Enforcement Notice?

Yes. The appeal must be lodged before the date mentioned on that notice. The possible grounds of appeal are set out in the Act and consist largely of negative statements such as that the building is not of special architectural or historic interest.

Enforcement Notices usually come after long and often unpleasant dealings with the Local Authority. If you are wise you will not let matters reach this stage. Asking first is always sensible and can save much annoyance, time and money.

What do I do if consent is refused?

You can appeal. In such cases, it is often a good idea to talk to the Planning Officer who dealt with your application. They may be able to tell you where you went wrong and whether there are any changes to your proposals which will make them acceptable. If you still want to appeal, it is a good idea to get professional advice for the appeal procedure can be complicated and expensive (see Chapter 4).

Is there any compensation for a refusal?

If you feel that without the Listed Building Consent the land or building cannot be put to any "reasonably beneficial use" then you could serve a "Listed Building Purchase Notice" on the Local Authority. This requires the Authority to buy the building or land from you. Such a course of action is also open to you if you feel that conditions put on a consent have the same effect. In practice it is difficult to prove that no "reasonably beneficial use" is possible. Successful claims are rare.

Can anything happen to overturn a consent?

Yes. The Local Authority has power to revoke or modify a Listed Building Consent which it has already given, but this must be confirmed by the Secretary of State for the Environment. The Secretary of State can also revoke or modify a consent. In each case a notice must be served on the owner, occupier and anyone else who may have an interest. This notice gives up to twenty eight days for them to make representations to the Secretary of State.

If such a thing happens, then the owner etc can put in a claim for compensation if there has been abortive work done and they have sustained loss or damage. Fortunately such cases are extremely rare.

Ancient Monuments

In a few, rare cases a Listed Building may also be "Scheduled" as an "Ancient Monument". This is done under a different Act:- "The Ancient Monuments and Archaeological Areas Act 1979". In this Act the Secretary of State for National Heritage is required to prepare Schedules of Ancient Monuments in a similar way to the preparation of the lists of buildings.

Ancient Monuments are protected by their own legislation which takes precedence over the Listed Building legislation. Thus, if you have a building which is scheduled as well as being listed, you would need to get Scheduled Monument Consent for any works rather than Listed Building Consent.
It is important to know that Listing and Scheduling are two different things. They are often confused. There is no such thing as a scheduled ancient building or a listed monument!

If you have any doubts about whether the building is an Ancient Monument, your Local Authority should be able to help. County Councils are required to keep a register of such monuments for members of the public to look at, and most Local Councils will also know which parts of their areas are scheduled.

Applications for Ancient Monument Consent must be made to the Secretary of State and you should write to :- HSD3, Room 242, Lambeth Bridge House, Albert Embankment, London, SE1 7SB.

Chapter Three

How Do I Apply for
Listed Building Consent?

Chapter Three
How Do I Apply for Listed Building Consent?

Before you submit the application

First consider exactly what you want to have done to the building. Keep in mind that, whilst you are applying for consent to do works which are "likely to affect the character of the building", you will be expected still to respect that character.

Section 16 of the Act requires the Local Authority or Secretary of State to have "special regard to the desirability of preserving the building or its setting or any features of special architectural or historic interest". This gives you some idea of what will be moving the thoughts of the various people you deal with.

Informal Advice

When you have some idea of what you want to do, contact the Conservation Officer or Area Planning Officer of your Local Council and make an appointment to discuss your proposals. Take with you some photographs of the relevant parts of the building and rough sketches of what you want to do. You will receive informal advice on what may be acceptable. This will eliminate complete non-starters at an early stage, saving you time and money.

It is possible that the Officer may agree to a site visit, which is the most helpful way of gaining good advice. Be prepared to be flexible. Remember that the Officer is there to help you, but he or she is also there to look after the character of the building.

It is best that pre-application advice is spoken rather than written. Written comments are likely to be less flexible and may amount to a hasty consideration of your proposal. This could affect the formal consideration of the actual application.

Specialists

If you have a Grade II* or Grade I building, be prepared for other specialists to be called in, such as representatives of English Heritage. You may find yourself engulfed in a crowd of "experts" all apparently discussing your building as if they owned it. Try not to take offence at this. It is done with the best of intentions and can prove an invaluable source of free information and advice.

Your Agent

It will help if you have your professional representative, such as an architect, but try to make sure that your professional is skilled in dealing with historic buildings. Not all architects, surveyors etc have the necessary specialised knowledge. Your Local Authority may be able to give you some names and addresses of local specialists.

Even if you have a representative, make your own notes of what happens at meetings which you attend. If you cannot do it at the actual meeting do it straight afterwards while you can still remember properly what has been said. This should be done throughout the whole process of the application and especially for any site meetings. It is easy to get interested in what is being said about the building and forget to take notes.

You will also need to take notes of what your representative tells you.

Site Meetings

Beware of meetings on site which split into two or three groups. This can give rise to misunderstandings, since no-one can know what is happening in all the groups. Try to keep everyone together.

Submitting the Application

The next stage is to produce drawings of the work proposed and fill in the application forms.

This is best done by a specialist, but you need to know the type of thing which will be required so that you can check and comment on what your specialist produces.

Drawings etc (see examples in the Appendix)

The number of drawings depends on the extent and complexity of the work.

- **As existing**

    What will be needed first are drawings showing the building as it is now, before the alterations. These may be referred to as survey drawings. They should, at least, consist of plans and elevations.

- **Archaeological and Record Surveys**

  If you want to do major works, or alterations to a timber frame, or your building is Grade II* or Grade I, you may need to have an "archaeological" survey and report done. This does not mean digging up the garden, but a very full and careful measured survey of the building's structure. This must be done by a specialist.It may seem expensive and time consuming, but, in the long run, it is a wise measure. You will then know what you have historically and structurally in your building. Consequently you can make more informed and sensible decisions on what should be done. You can save money and time later on by ensuring that the structure is not endangered by the work proposed. These "archaeological" drawings will include plans, elevations, sections and details at a large scale. There should also be a report explaining what the building consists of and how it has evolved.

- **As Proposed**

  Next you need drawings "as proposed". These again will depend on the work to be done. The minimum is plans and elevations, but you may also need sections and details to a larger scale of such items as staircases, windows etc if they are to be altered.

- **Site Plan**

  Along with these drawings a Site Plan of not less than 1:2500 scale will be needed showing the site and its surroundings. This is so that the right site is considered.

- **Block Plan**

  You may also need a Block Plan of 1:500 scale to show the relationship of extensions, or drainage to the building, the site and the surroundings.

- **Photographs**

  It also helps to provide photographs of all elevations of the building and for any part of the interior which may be affected. Where demolition is proposed, photographs are essential.

- **Application Forms**

  You will need to obtain Application Forms from your Local Authority and fill them in. This can be done by your representative if you wish. If you have any problems, staff at the Local Authority will help you.

What are the Application Forms like?

Each Local Authority produces its own forms, usually with an accompanying explanatory leaflet. The Appendix includes an example of a form. We will consider each question separately.

Questions 1 & 2:-   Names and Addresses of Applicant and Agent.

Anyone can make an application for consent on a building, whether they own it or not, but, if they do not own the building they must notify the owner.

If you have a professional representative, you may ask them to be your agent. If you fill in this part of the form, all the correspondence will be sent to their address.

In the absence of an agent remember to give your daytime telephone number.

Question 3:-   a)   Building Location

This will be the address of the building which is the subject of your application.

b)   Building Use

This is the current use of the building, or if vacant, the last use. eg House

c)   Listed Grade

This is the grade I, II* or II which you will find on the list.

Question 4:-   What is the application for?

This should be a simple description of what you want to do. Be careful to mention any demolitions. e.g. remove wall between living room and kitchen. State whether the proposal involves:-

Alteration - e.g. replacement windows

Extension - e.g. an extra room or two added on. (You may also need planning permission)

Demolition - e.g. removing any part of the structure is demolition.

Question 5:-   List of all drawings submitted, with their reference numbers.

Question 6:-   Your interests in the land e.g owner or tenant.

Question 7:-   Other proposals on the site. e.g. you might want to build a detached garage. (You may also need planning permission)

DO NOT FORGET TO SIGN AND DATE THE FORMS.

Usually four copies of the forms are required. You will need to make sure that they are all filled in completely and each question is answered in the same way. Each form must be signed and dated.

Certificate of Ownership

Along with the application forms you should receive copies of a certificate of ownership. If you own and occupy the site, then you simply sign and date the form. If you do not own the site, then you must notify the owner and fill in the appropriate part of the certificate.

REMEMBER TO KEEP A COPY OF EVERYTHING SUBMITTED AND OF ALL LETTERS AND NOTICES SENT TO YOU.

Further Consultations

If the application includes demolition, then the Local Authority must notify the following bodies and consider their comments:-

> The Ancient Monument Society
> The Council for British Archaeology
> The Georgian Group
> The Society for the Protection of Ancient Buildings
> The Victorian Society
> The Royal Commission on Historic Monuments

In this case they may ask you for extra copies of drawings and photographs.

If the application is for a Grade II* or I building, the Secretary of State and the Historic Buildings and Monuments Commission for England (English Heritage), or the Welsh Office for Wales must also be notified. If he is so minded the Secretary of State can then call in the application for his own decision. If permission for demolition is given you will be required to notify the Royal Commission on Historic Monuments before demolition takes place and to give their staff the opportunity to record what is to be demolished.

Do I need to apply for Planning Permission as well?

If the work which you intend to do would have required planning permission on an ordinary, unlisted building, then you will also need planning permission for your Listed Building.

Listed Building Consent is an extra control over and above planning permission. One consolation is that you do not have to pay a fee for Listed Building Consent, even though a fee is required for planning permission.

What happens to the application now?

- First the application will be checked to make sure that the forms are properly completed and all the necessary drawings and photographs are included.

- Then the application will be registered and given a number. You should be sent an acknowledgement of receipt telling you that number.

- Sets of documents will be sent to the various bodies who have to be consulted and the Parish or Town Council will be notified.

- The application must be advertised. A notice will be displayed on the site for not less than seven days saying what is intended and inviting comments, which have to be given to the Local Authority within twenty one days. A similar notice will be published in a local newspaper. The Local Authority is bound to consider these comments when determining your application. If the work only affects the interior of a Grade II building this does not have to be advertised on site.

- A Planning Officer will be allocated to your application, usually someone who specialises in historic buildings. If you have an application for planning permission as well, then there may be two officers dealing with your applications, one looking at it from the planning side of things and one from the Listed Buildings point of view. In complicated cases, a consultant, either from the County Council or a private consultancy may also be involved.

- These Officers will need to visit the site. It is important that they do this, for even the best drawings cannot entirely explain what the building is actually like and how it relates to its surroundings.

- They may ask for changes to the proposal if they feel that there are problems which can be overcome. The officer in charge will, after all consultations have been received, make a recommendation of refusal or approval.

- The decision will be made by the Chief Officer responsible for planning matters, or the application will be considered by a Planning Committee made up of Local Councillors. If objections are raised as a result of the consultations it is likely that the application will be taken to a committee. The Planning Committee may make a site visit prior to making a decision.

The Decision

You will be issued with a Decision Notice which will tell you whether or not consent has been given.

Conditions

If consent is given, the decision will be subject to conditions. It is important that you read these carefully and make sure that your builder knows about them and has the latest copies of the drawings. If you or your builder do not comply with the conditions you will commit a criminal offence.

There is usually a good reason for conditions and their imposition may have been the only way in which you would have got consent.

Section 17 of the Act gives the Authorities power to impose conditions on a consent and gives examples:-

"a)   the preservation of particular features of the building either as part of it or after severance from it.

b)   the making good, after works are completed, of any damage caused to the building by the works.

c)   the reconstruction of the building or any part of it following the execution of any works, with the use of original materials so far as practicable and with such alterations of the interior of the building as may be specified in the conditions."

A condition can also be imposed requiring that specified details of the work be submitted and approved by the Planning Authority at a later date.

In the case of demolition there may be a condition requiring that the building is not demolished until a contract for redevelopment work has been let and planning permission for that work has been given.

If you do not agree with the conditions you can either apply for relaxation by making a further Listed Building Consent application, or appeal against them to the Secretary of State for the Environment.

How long does all this take?

The minimum length of time is determined by the number of consultations and the cycle of Planning Committee meetings. Local Authorities have a duty to determine applications within eight weeks, but, with Listed Building Consent Applications, it can take longer.

The decision may be delayed beyond eight weeks where there are adverse comments and alterations need to be made to the drawings to overcome them. Whatever the need, do not start work until you have the written consent otherwise you may commit an offence.

Is there any time limit to a consent?

Yes. Listed Building consents are granted subject to works having begun within five years of the date of issue of the consent. If you cannot start within that time it is possible to apply for renewal, but this must be done before the time limit expires.

In some cases the Authority may put a shorter time limit on and, where this is the case, you may not get agreement to a renewal.

Chapter Four

Appealing against a
Refusal or Conditions

Chapter Four
Appealing against a refusal, or conditions

What can I appeal against?

You may appeal if:-

- Your application has been refused.

- You do not accept a condition which has been attached to an approval.

- The Local Authority has not made a decision on your application within eight weeks. This type of appeal is usually used by people who know their application will be refused and wish to lodge an appeal as soon as possible.

Should I appeal?

First read the decision notice carefully, making sure you understand the reasons given for refusal. Find out exactly what the problems are by talking to the Planning Officer involved.

Find out whether your application was considered by the Planning Committee. If it was, was it recommended for approval by the Planning Officer? When the Committee goes against the advice of its officers it may be worth appealing, for in those cases the issues can be finely balanced.

• Cost	An influential factor in reaching the decision to go to appeal is cost. While there is no fee to be paid for appeals, there is the cost of your own time to consider and of any professional advice which you may need.
• Time	Time is also important. Making an appeal is likely to take at least six months, and could take up to a year, depending on the type of appeal and the complexities of the case.
• Your Case	Consider these points carefully before you start the process. Make sure that you have a very clear idea of what your case is. Your case must cover the issue of the preservation of the character of the building and its special architectural or historic interest.

• The Issues   You will need to show clearly and convincingly that what you want to do will not harm the character of the building or its setting.

A specific ground for appeal, sometimes used where the building is subject to a Building Preservation Notice is that you do not agree that the building is of "Special Architectural or Historic Interest" and that it should be removed from the List. You need to be very sure of your arguments to do this and will almost certainly need specialised advice and the opinions of experts to back you up.

Who decides the outcome of the Appeal?

Listed Building Consent appeals are considered by Inspectors appointed by the Secretary of State for the Environment. The Inspectors make recommendations to the Secretary of State who then decides.

What are the types of Appeal?

There are three kinds of appeal process.

- Written Representations

- Informal Hearings

- Public Inquiries

You may request any one of these.

In most cases written representation appeals will be the most appropriate.

The Local Authority must agree with your choice. If there is any dispute, the Department of the Environment will decide.

Either side can insist on a Public Inquiry.

How do I appeal?

On the back of the decision notice or on a separate sheet will be the address of the Department of the Environment office which deals with appeals. Contact them and they will send the relevant forms.

You must appeal within six months of issue of the decision notice or within six months following the expiry of the eight week period, whichever is the sooner. You must provide copies of the following documents as part of your appeal:

- The application

- The relevant plans, drawings and documents submitted with the application

- The notice of decision, if any

- All other correspondence with the Local Planning Authority

The procedures are as follows:-

Written Representations Appeals

You make a written statement saying what your case is and why permission should have been granted. The Local Authority makes a written statement also. You then exchange the statements and have a chance to comment on each other's point of view.

A Planning Inspector is given the statements with any extra factual background information and letters of objection and support from interested parties. He or she will then make a site visit. You will be told when this is to take place so that you can be present. No discussion of the case is permitted at this time.

After consideration, the Inspector tells the Secretary of State his or her opinion. The decision is made and you are informed by letter.

Informal Hearing Appeals

Written statements are exchange as above and you are entitled to see the Local Authority's case before you submit your own. The hearing consists of a meeting between yourself (with or without your agent), a representative of the Local Planning Authority, a Planning Inspector and any other interested person.

The proposal will be discussed. A site visit will be made and the Inspector may continue the discussions on site. The Inspector will then go away and consider what he or she has heard and make a recommendation to the Secretary of State as before.

Public Inquiry Appeals

The procedure is very formal and can be intimidating to the uninitiated. It is usual for both sides to be represented by solicitors and barristers or other advocates. You may also need to employ specialists in historic buildings and planning.

Statements of case are read by witnesses and each side has the opportunity of cross-examining the other and of making a final summing up.

Public Inquiries are usually reserved for large developments, major works to Grade II* or Grade I buildings or complicated cases involving unauthorised developments.

Will the Planning Department help me with the appeal?

You have the right to see public documents relating to your application and details of any other Listed Building or Planning applications which have been made in the past. Before appealing it is always useful to find out the planning history of your site and of other similar buildings in the area.

The Planning Department of the Local Authority has the duty to help you with your appeal in this way, even though you may be appealing against their refusal.

What if I lose the appeal?

The decision letter will clearly set out the reasons for the decision. It may be that you can overcome these by changes to your proposal e.g. by reducing the height of an extension. If this is the case you can apply again with a new or amended scheme.

You can only challenge the decision on a point of law. Any challenge must be made through the high court, where expensive legal representation will be needed.

The Ombudsman

If you feel strongly that the Planning Authority has not followed correct procedures in dealing with your application, you can make a complaint to the Ombudsman. It is important to remember that the Ombudsman only deals with the correct use of administrative procedures. He will not be interested in the professional judgement of the Planning Officers.

Further information about the work of the Ombudsman is available from:-

The Secretary
Commission for Local Administration for England
21 Queen Anne's Gate
London
SW1H 9BU

Chapter Five

Dereliction,
Grants and VAT

Chapter Five
Dereliction, Grants and VAT

Prevention of Deterioration and Damage

Chapter 5 of the 1991 Act covers "Prevention of Deterioration and Damage". This section of the Act give the Local Councils power to deal with the effects of a building being left without maintenance or deliberately neglected.

If a Listed Building is allowed to fall into disrepair, then the Local Authority, or the Secretary of State, has the power to require repairs to be done. As a last resort they can compulsorily purchase the building.

There are two kinds of action which can be taken:-

Unoccupied Buildings

In the case of an unoccupied building, a notice can be served requiring the owner to carry out urgent repairs. Those repairs must be the minimum to keep the building standing and wind and weather tight. The notice will specify the repairs necessary for this.

Such a notice can also be served to cover the unoccupied part of a building which is partly occupied.

If the repairs are not done by the owner within the time limit given, then the Authority may do the repairs and recover the costs from the owner. These costs can include continuing expenses, such as the hire of scaffolding.

The owner can, within 28 days of service of the notice, make a case to the Secretary of State that:-

- Some or all of the work is unnecessary for the preservation of the building.

- Where it is a case of temporary support or shelter, the arrangements have continued for an unreasonable length of time.

- That the amount specified in the notice is unreasonable.

- That the recovery of the amount would cause the owner hardship.

Occupied Buildings

Where a building is occupied, a **Repairs Notice** may be served.

This is considered to be the first step to compulsory purchase by the authority which has served the notice. This kind of notice must specify the works considered reasonably necessary for the proper preservation of the building. It may include more work than the urgent repairs mentioned above.

Compulsory Purchase

Three months after the service of the repairs notice, if the work has not been done, the authority can start proceedings for compulsory purchase.

If the authority does not start proceedings, then the owner can serve a Listed Building Purchase Notice on the authority concerned.

Section 50 of the Act allows the authority which hopes to buy the building by compulsory purchase, to pay only minimum compensation if it can be proved that the building has been deliberately left to go derelict.

These powers are not used by Local Authorities as often as you might expect because they are time consuming and expensive. If the Authority finally purchases a building it must then repair the building and find a use for it. Usually, if a building seems to be falling into disrepair, the officers of the authority will contact the owner and discuss matters, perhaps to offer help by way of grants or advice. Urgent works or repair notices are looked on as a final resort.

Local Authority Grants and Loans

Section 57 of the Act gives the Local Authorities the power to make grants or loans towards the cost of repair or maintenance of Listed Buildings in their area. It also allows them to contribute towards unlisted buildings which they consider to be of architectural or historic interest.

It does not say that they must contribute. Consequently, if money is set aside for such grants or loans, it can easily be cut out of the budget of a hard pressed Council, which may look on Listed Buildings as a low priority when money is in short supply.
Many Authorities who once gave help no longer do so. All that can be said is that in some cases grants or loans may be available from the Local Authority towards repair and maintenance.

Other Funds

In the case of buildings graded II* and I there is another possibility for financial help towards repairs. That is English Heritage (the Welsh Office in Wales), which has its own budget for this purpose. This budget is to cover the whole country so there is again every chance that, having applied, you will find that there is little or nothing available.

Improvement Grants

If you are in the situation where you may be eligible for a grant under the Housing Acts, commonly known as "improvement grants", then owning a Listed Building can be useful. Extra money is available for any special works required.

It is important, when applying for such a grant, to let the officers dealing with it know that the building is listed and also to let the Listed Buildings section of the Planning Department know, for some of the works asked for in connection with the grant may require Listed Building Consent.

Free Advice

What is useful is the specialised advice available both from Local Authority Staff and English Heritage or the Welsh Office.

If you have a problem about repair and maintenance, asking for help is always worthwhile. If they cannot solve your problem they will put you in touch with another specialist who may be able to help.

VAT Exemptions

Another possible advantage of owning a Listed Building at present lies in the VAT laws.

Works for the alteration of a Listed Building which have received Listed Building Consent are not liable for VAT. Unfortunately works of repair are liable for VAT payments, so the advantage is small. There is no guarantee that this situation will continue.

Conclusion

Other than the pleasure of owning and using an interesting, historic building, the advantages for the individual owner of a Listed Building are few.

The law is drawn up from the point of view of the whole of society rather than the individual. We all like to see old and interesting buildings well looked after, but as individuals we do not necessarily want to take the responsibility for them.

Chapter Six

Living with a
Listed Building

Chapter Six
Living with a Listed Building

Living with the Building, not in it.

The title of this book has been chosen carefully to express a particular way of dealing with old buildings. Living **with** them rather than **in** them is the safest and simplest way of preserving the building as well as the sanity of the owner. Before doing anything to the building you need to know it well. Watch it over at least one set of seasons. In this way you can avoid doing unnecessary, and possibly abortive work.

Every past owner and occupier of the building will have tried to imprint their own character on the building in the form of repair, alterations and additions. During that time the building itself will have achieved its own character, strengths and weaknesses, becoming an amalgamation of past ideas.

Old buildings and old people have a lot in common. They are fascinating in what they can tell us of the past, but they are perhaps a little frail and set in their ways. Changing them may be difficult, if not impossible. You need to go along with them. They need love, care, attention and, above all, understanding. Old buildings cannot and should not be expected to provide the same standards of comfort as new buildings. Prospective owners should be prepared to allow for minor changes in their lifestyles to accommodate this.

• Respect

It is necessary to respect the age and character of the building and remember that every alteration and addition is a valid part of the life of the building and a link with its previous occupants.

• Understanding

In the movement towards knowing your building, it helps to find out what might have happened to it in the past and how it fits into the historical patterns of building construction and use. This is beyond the scope of the present book, but there are other books dealing with such matters. In some areas there are evening classes dealing with the history of buildings. If you have a small house, look for any which cover "vernacular architecture".

• Care

While you are "learning" your building you will need to keep it maintained. This is an important matter. You will not only be protecting your investment but, if done properly, saving money in the future. If the building is well maintained little repair should be necessary. The purpose of most buildings is to protect their users from the elements. The most destructive of these is water. The usual causes of water entering are leaky roofs, rising damp or faulty drainage.

The purpose of repair and maintenance is to restrain the inevitable processes of decay without damage to the character of the building. Intervention should, therefore, be kept to a minimum, with any repairs being done in a traditional manner, replacing like with like.

N.B. Modern building methods and materials are not always compatible with old buildings and their use can sometimes cause irreparable damage. In some cases you will find that the more you do to the building the worse you can make it, so think carefully before you act.

The Key Principles

The way most listed buildings are constructed and the materials used in them allow for natural movements responding to seasonal changes of temperature and humidity.

In repair and maintenance to the majority of listed buildings there are two rules, which need to be followed.

1. The building must be able to move freely with the seasons.

2. There must be ventilation to allow moisture to evaporate and the building to "breathe".

Regular Maintenance

Assuming the building is in reasonable condition when you acquire it, a regular, simple programme of inspection and maintenance can be put into effect from the beginning.

Maintenance Checklist

At regular intervals take a brief walk round the building. Check on the following:-

- **Roof**   Are there any slipping tiles or slates?
              Is the thatch tight and tidy?
              Are any flashings still in place?
              In a building with a lead roof, is all the lead still there?

- **Rainwater Goods**   Are the gutters clear and the joints tight? There should be no leaks.
  Are the rainwater pipes working properly, without cracks and leaks?
  Is the water getting away at the bottom?
  Look for signs of water staining behind rainwater pipes and below gutters (green or brown stains) or for unnaturally clean areas of wall.

- **Walls**   If the walls are rendered note any cracks and areas of loose render. With other walls also, if there are cracks, keep an eye on them and note how they move. Sometimes cracks open and close with the seasons. Sometimes buildings move once, crack and do not move again.
  Look at the base of the walls to make sure that any vents are clear. Check that the soil level is not creeping up above any damp proof courses or timber framing. Check that no overflows are overflowing.

- **Windows and Doors**   Is there any cracked or missing glass?
  Are they properly painted?
  Is there any missing or cracked putty?
  If leaded lights, are the leads well fitted and not sagging?

Make sure you know exactly where stop cocks and electric switches are and that they are working properly in case of emergency.

This is a "stich in time" method. By doing this regularly you can catch trouble before it has time to cause major damage.

Don't Panic

Most Listed Buildings have survived for many years, so there is rarely need to act hastily.

If there are any problems look for the cause and try to put that right rather than the symptoms.

Replace where needed with the same kind of materials and building methods as were used in the existing building. Don't be tempted to use cheap short cuts, they usually cause more trouble in the long run.

Each building has its owner danger points which you will become aware of and can add to your check lists.

It helps to form a habit of looking over the building as you come home from work etc.

This is a simple but effective way of keeping your building standing. The following chapters give a little more detail on some of these points.

Extending a Listed Building

Listed Buildings are not frozen in time. Buildings have always been changed in the past and it is often the accumulation of these changes which gives a building its special character. Even today, it is not impossible to add to an old building while keeping that character. Some buildings are such complete examples of their type or design that extending them can be very difficult without losing that completeness.

- **Siting**

  The way a building is set on its site and how it looks in relation to nearby buildings are part of its character. This is why the "Listing" includes the curtilage of the building.

  In extending a building you need to keep in mind what the whole site looks like from both near and far. Try walking around the neighbourhood and looking at your building from a distance. Your extension should not stand out in the views of the older building.

- **Main parts of the building**

  Although the law covers all of a Listed Building and its curtilage, there are often particular elevations or blocks, which are older or more consciously designed than others. These need to be identified and avoided when you are adding on an extension.

  In designing an extension you need to be aware, not only of your needs, but also of the special character of your building, so that the old building will still be the main element on the site.

- **Design**

  The design of your extension should be sympathetic to the Listed Building, but need not copy it. Modern designs can be just as successful as exact copies, if they take the character of the existing building and its siting into account.

  You will soon come across words used in describing design, which are technical terms to cover ideas used in designing a building or extension, but difficult to explain.

  Here are a few, which we will try to explain.

Element:	Part of a building. This can be a whole block or a window or door. The "dominant element on the site" would be the "Main Block" mentioned above.
Scale:	Usually used to mean the relationship of the size of the building to a human being.
Proportions:	The relationship of parts of a building to the whole. For example, the relationship of the shape of a window opening to the shape of the whole wall.

Harmony: The feeling of "rightness" which comes when the parts of a building agree together, giving a suitable, and often comforting, effect.

All these need to be looked at with the existing building in mind when you are designing an extension. Matching the scale and proportions of an extension to those of the existing building will help to make the two look right together, and so produce harmony in the design.

- **Materials**

   The materials chosen for an extension will also have an effect on the way it looks. They need not always match exactly but should, at least, complement the existing building.

- **Rules**

   The main rule in extending a Listed Building is to keep the particular character of the building in mind and always defer to that in your design. Every case is different, for every building is different.

   Other, more detailed rules, which may be quoted to you, such as "the extension must be of a lower height than the existing building," can usually be boiled down to variations of getting the scale and proportions right. Such rules are only indications of ways of arriving at harmony. If they are rigidly applied then the chance to produce something exciting and interesting may be lost.

Be realistic

Treat the old building as the special thing it is, and remember that there are limits to what can be done. Any building must be suitable to its purpose. You cannot expect small cottages to be able to provide vast amounts of living space.

If you keep the rules of scale and proportion in mind you will see that small buildings will only happily accept small extensions.

Think out what your needs are and look for a building which will meet them with the least amount of change. "Falling in love with a building", or other romantic ideas often lead to disappointment.

Chapter Seven

The Roof

Chapter Seven
The Roof

The first line of defence against water is the roof. The roof consists of a waterproof covering supported on a timber, or less frequently, metal or stone structure. If the roof covering works, then the structure will be unlikely to fail, unless it is altered without due thought to its purpose.

Potential Problems with Roof Coverings.

Roof coverings commonly found on old buildings are, thatch, clay tiles, stone tiles or slates and lead. All these, if properly installed and maintained will last for many years. There are two main problem points. One is the fixing of these onto the roof structure and the other is the junctions between slopes of the roof and abutments with other buildings, chimneys, walls and parapets.

Fixing the Roof Covering.

The fixing of all these materials, except lead is similar. They are fixed onto timber laths which are nailed onto rafters. If water gets in, these nails can rust and the roof covering slide off.

Should this be your problem, beware of short cuts like applying substances to the underside of the roof to stick the structure together. This can seal the whole structure, preventing the roof from "breathing" by stopping the water which is coming in from getting out. This water will be held against the rafters and they will rot. You will then have to replace the whole roof structure rather than simply stripping and re-fixing what is already there.

Tiles or Slates

Clay tiles and stone tiles or slates are hung on the laths with pegs put through holes in the tiles or slates. Pegs can be made of animal bone, wood, iron and more lately, galvanised iron and plastic.

If the pegs fail or the tiles break at the holes, the tiles or slates will slip off the roof.

During the 19th and early 20th Centuries iron pegs or nails were used. These tend to rust over time and cause tiles and slates to slip.

- **Slipping tiles and slates**

  The first signs of trouble are odd tiles or slates slipping out of place. These can be put back individually by temporarily hanging them on pieces of lead called tingles.

  Don't leave it. When you first notice slipping slates or tiles, put the odd tiles back on and begin to consider re-roofing.

  The only safe answer to the problem is to remove the roof covering and re-hang it with new oak pegs or galvanised nails.

  Sometimes the slates or tiles may be cracked by expansion which happens with rusting metal. In this case you will need to find some similar slates or tiles to replace the damaged ones.

- **Wind**

  With overlapping materials like slates and tiles there is a problem with wind blowing rain or snow between them. The old builders solved this either by bedding the tiles on straw or moss or by pointing the joints inside the roof with lime mortar (torching). The modern form of this is laying the tiles or slates on roofing felt. If you decide to use felt in re-roofing, remember to allow for some ventilation to the space below the roof covering so that condensation does not happen in the roof space.

- **Pointing**

  If you decide to have a stone tiled roof pointed internally as was done in the past, remember that the mortar mix must be similar to that used in the old pointing. It is not a good idea to point tiled or slated roofs on the outside or inside with cement mortar or with modern mastics. This seals in water and stops the roof from moving with the seasons.

- **Bitumous Coverings**

  Using bituminous coverings on tiles or slates is also unwise. These stick closely to the surface of the tiles or slates so that, if water gets underneath, it cannot get out. In this case, either the timbers underneath begin to decay or the water in the tiles freezes, expands and causes them to break up. What appears to be a quick repair, can cause more trouble and may result in the loss of the whole roof covering.

Thatch

Thatching is the covering of roofs with vegetable material such as straw, water reeds, heather etc. It helps to remember that, while thatch might be expensive today, it was the cheapest material available in the past.

People who used thatch for their roof coverings in the past expected to have to give it regular maintenance. It was part of the normal seasonal work to check and repair the thatch on roofs.

Modern owners of thatched roofs also need to give them regular maintenance. You may like to consider arranging for a thatcher to come once a year to do running maintenance. You can then catch problems early and lengthen the life of the roof. Since thatching materials were grown locally, they differ from place to place. The most common are water reed and corn straw. These are each put on the roof in different ways and so look different when installed. It is quite possible that you will be required to obtain Listed Building Consent if, for example, you replace longstraw with water reed, for this could change the character of the building.

- **Local Materials and Methods**

  It is best therefore, to use the local material and method of thatching, even though some materials may be said to last longer than others. Whatever is said, you need to remember that the life of a thatched roof is directly related to the care and maintenance given it.

- **The Ridge**

  The most vulnerable part of a thatched roof is the ridge. This protects the top of the rafters. Keep a regular eye on it so that any necessary repair is done quickly.

  The ridge can be renewed without completely re-thatching, but be careful that the design of the new ridge is the same as the old one, for changing the design of the ridge may alter the character of the building and consequently need Listed Building Consent.

- **Re-thatching**

  When you are told that the roof needs re-thatching, remember that this does not necessarily mean taking off the whole thatch down to the rafters. If the roof has been well looked after in the past, only the top weathered coat will need replacing. In some cases the base coat of thatch will have survived for hundreds of years and may even be covered with soot from the open fires used in early houses.

- **Soot**

  If the inside of your thatch is sooted then you have a very old house. Consult your Local Authority if it is thought necessary to remove all the thatch from such a building, for you will almost certainly need Listed Building Consent.

Junctions and Abutments

Junctions and abutments are treated similarly with all the roof coverings.

In cheaper constructions, a fillet, or strip of mortar is placed across the joint between the roof covering and the chimney or wall against which the roof is built. This is fine as long as the fillet is replaced regularly. If the fillet is left too long it will dry out and cracks will appear between it and the wall or roof. Water will get into the cracks and attack the roof structure. Your first sign of this may be a wet ceiling or worse. This is why in most buildings, where the money was available, lead was used to cover such junctions. These lead covers are called flashings.

Lead

Lead is used for gutters behind parapets and in valleys between differing roof slopes. It is also used as a covering for very low pitched roofs. It must be fully supported underneath, usually with boarding.

Lead is a wonderful material, for if properly looked after, it will last around a hundred years. When it needs to be replaced it can be melted down and re-cast. The main problem with lead is that it expands and contracts with heat and cold, so sheets both for flashing and roofing must not be too big and joints must allow for movement.

Small holes and cuts can occur from the mechanical action of people walking over lead roofs or gutters. So be careful if you go up to your roof to clear gutters. Working with lead is a job for a specialist known as a plumber. The word "plumber" means worker in lead.

Beware of D.I.Y. repairs with solder, bitumen etc. These contaminate the lead and make it unsuitable for re-use.

Roof Structure

Most roof structures are either completely made of timber or include some timber as direct support for the roof covering.

Timber is an organic material which will move with the seasons. This must be expected and allowed for. The older methods of growing and cutting the timber for building took this into account. Consequently, old timber structures will stand a lot of abuse before they finally have to submit to major repairs. The roof structure is there to support the roof covering so the heavier the roof covering, the sturdier the structure will be.

The weight is first transferred to rafters. These are inclined timbers joined at the top and held up by the walls at the bottom. There is a tendency for the feet of rafters to move apart under the weight of the roof covering, so horizontal timbers (tie beams) are usually put between them every so often to stop this happening. Beware of temptation to cut such timbers in order to give headroom in roof spaces or upper storeys. This will put the whole outward thrust of the roof onto the walls which will probably move outwards.

While alterations may have been done in the past, and the building may have suffered them without harm, today such an alteration would certainly require Listed Building Consent, if only to ensure that the consequences of the action had been thought about first.

Cleaning and Treatment

As mentioned under 'thatch' some early roofs have a coating of soot inside them caused by years of fires built on open hearths. This is important evidence of the history of the building and it should not be cleaned off. With a sooted roof it is essential to make sure that the structure is kept dry, so beware of suggestions that the roof should be sprayed with chemicals to prevent insect attack. If the roof is dry and ventilated such treatment should not be necessary.

Sapwood is the outer part of the tree. Heartwood is the centre of the tree. Most wood boring insects attack the sapwood and leave the heartwood alone, unless it has become wet. Consequently, if your building timber is more heartwood than sapwood it is less likely to suffer from insect attack. The traditional way of cutting timber made sure that there was as little sapwood as possible in the building.

In some cheap 18th Century roofs, you may find rafters made of coppice poles about 75mm (3") in diameter, with the bark still on them. These have a great deal of sapwood in them and are prone to attack by furniture beetle (woodworm). In this case you may wish to consider some form of treatment, but take advice from an independent specialist first.

One thing to remember when dealing with the inside of roofs, is that there are now laws drawn up to preserve bats. If you have bats, be careful and take advice, for disturbing them can be an offence and any chemical treatments must not hurt them.

Tradesmen

Where you need to have work done in the roof space by tradesmen such as electricians or plumbers, make sure that they are warned that the house is Listed and that they are aware that cutting or chasing of timbers, or breaking through partitions may need Listed Building Consent.

Make sure that you are told exactly where they need to go to do their work and what alterations to the building are needed, however small these seem, so that you can check this out with the Local Planning Authority before work begins.

As a rule, chasing and cutting of old structural timbers should be avoided because this may cause structural movement as well as removing historic evidence. You may have to learn to live with visible wiring and plumbing simply to ensure that the building remains standing.

Chapter Eight

Rainwater, Drainage and Damp

Chapter Eight
Rainwater Drainage and Damp

The roof covering protects the roof structure from the rain. This is important because the roof structure is usually a material which is likely to be attacked by fungus or insects if it gets wet. When the rainwater is brought to the edge of the roof, it must be taken to the ground without being allowed to damage the walls.

Thatched Roofs

With thatched roofs this is done by having a wide overhang at the eaves so that the water is thrown well clear of the walls.

If you have a thatched roof, the area beneath the overhang needs to be kept clear and dry. It is preferable to have a gravelled area, so that water run off can drain easily away. If it is paved in any way make sure the paving slopes away from the building so that the water runs away from the base of the walls.

Other Roofs

With other roofs the rain is removed by rainwater gutters leading to spouts or rainwater pipes.

Rainwater gutters collect the water from the edge of the roof. They can easily become blocked by leaves and debris, causing water to overflow and damage the walls. Gutters should always be kept clean.

Parapet Gutters

In some cases the gutters are lead lined boxes, set behind parapet walls.

Parapet gutters can cause major problems if they are allowed to become blocked, or the lead is old, worn or punctured. Water can flow into the roof structure itself at the vital point where it is supported by the walls and can also enter the top of the walls.

Be aware of this possibility and make sure you have access to the parapet gutters and that they are kept clear, particularly around the outlets where they join the rainwater pipes.

Valley Gutters

Some roofs have more than one pitch. In these cases the junction between pitches forms a valley, which must be protected against water entry by lead sheeting. This is another danger point. Valley gutters can cause trouble, if they overflow or become blocked.

Where houses have square plans, there may be four roof pitches around a central valley. In this case there is a need to take rainwater from this valley to the outer edge of the roof. This is often done by lead lined box gutters taking the water through the roof space to an outlet at the edge of the roof.

These gutters should be inspected regularly, for if they become blocked or overflow, the water comes directly into the centre of the building to cause extreme damage to the structure. A well placed dead pigeon or bird's nest can cause many thousands of pounds of damage if ignored.

Gutters

The most usual form of gutter is a channel formed of metal such as cast iron. Again these gutters must be kept clear. They also need to be inspected regularly to ensure that the joints are good and that they are not cracked or rusted.

Stains on the walls below the gutters or worn areas on the ground will warn you of leaks.

Make sure they are kept properly painted. Cast iron rainwater goods should last a long time and should not rust if they are kept properly painted and maintained.

If you are starting off with a poorly maintained building, sort out the rainwater goods as soon as possible. Cast iron can be taken down, treated against rust, reinstalled and repainted.

You may think that this is expensive, but other materials are not as long lived and you will probably need Listed Building Consent to replace cast iron with other materials. You may even get a grant for keeping your cast iron.

Do not be tempted to mix cast iron and plastic rainwater goods except in desperate circumstances and as a temporary measure. They do not move together and the joints soon come apart.

Spouts

Spouts, sometimes called gargoyles, act like the thatch overhang to throw the water away from the walls. You need to make sure that they do this properly without the water hitting things on the ground and splashing back up onto the walls.

Rainwater Pipes

Rainwater pipes on old buildings are usually of lead or cast iron. They should also be kept clear and maintained. Stains or unnaturally clean patches on the walls behind or beside rainwater pipes are indicators of trouble.

- **Cast Iron**

  Apart from the joints, the usual place for rainwater pipes to give way is at the back against the wall. This tends to be the difficult place to paint and consequently it gets missed out allowing the cast iron pipes to rust. Run your fingers up behind the rainwater pipe. If it feels rough then it probably needs painting.

  The remarks about cast iron gutters also apply to rainwater pipes.

- **Lead**

  Lead tends to sag and crack with age, so beware pipes which are not straight or do not have smooth bends. You will probably need to get Listed Building Consent if you want to replace lead rainwater goods with another material. Remember that lead can be re-cast and re-used.

Ground Level Drainage

Having got the water from the roof to the ground it must then be taken away from the building. Just because your rainwater pipes disappear into the ground it doesn't mean that the water is taken away.

If you have damp patches on your walls, check whether they are near rainwater pipes.

Rainwater pipes should empty into drains which carry the water well away from the building. It is best for them to be connected to gullies. These give you the option of cleaning the drains from time to time. Always make sure that the gratings over the gullies are kept clear of leaves, earth and debris, which may block the drains.

If your rainwater pipes just disappear into the earth, clear gently around them to check whether they are connected to drains. Sometimes gullies get covered with earth, particularly where there are flower beds round the base of the walls.If the rainwater pipes just stop, then you need to consider putting in drains, but check with your Local Authority for you will need to comply with the Building Regulations. You may also need Listed Building Consent.

Damp and Heating

Most old buildings are used to a little dampness. It is excessive wetness that must be avoided. Complete drying out is not to be recommended. If you are thinking of installing central heating, be careful where the heat sources, e.g. radiators, are placed. Start the heating gradually to allow the building to get used to it. Sudden drying out, particularly of timber frames, can cause the building to start moving and may endanger the structure.

• **Rising Damp - Walls**

   Most timber frames and earth buildings are built with a base of whatever local stone is available so that the worst rising damp is avoided. Some later brick buildings will have the bottom of the wall made of more dense bricks and some may have a layer of slate set about 150mm (6") above the original ground level.

   Care should be taken not to cover up these base courses of the walls or the bottom members of the timber frames with earth. Flower beds at the base of the walls can be a particular problem.

• **Rising Damp - Floors**

   Early floors were mostly made of beaten earth. In places where suitable stone was readily available this was used for paving, but brick and tile floors, unless in very large expensive buildings belong to the 19th Century. In smaller houses the use of timber for ground floors is also a later addition, often with boarding being laid on thin joists directly onto the old earth floor.

   Where there are timber floors at ground floor level, it is best for the space beneath these to be ventilated. Often this is done by putting metal ventilation grilles in the base of walls. These grilles should never be blocked or covered.

   The fungus which attacks timber thrives in wet, unventilated spaces, so to avoid trouble, make sure that enclosed spaces in your building are well ventilated.

Damp Proof Courses

Removing old floors and replacing them with new solid floors including damp proof courses, can cause trouble by stopping the dampness from escaping through the floor and forcing it to find another way out, usually up the walls. Take advice before replacing floors in this way. You may also be removing historic evidence by taking out the old floor, so Listed Building Consent would probably be required.

A popular course of action in damp buildings is to put damp proof courses into the base of walls. In some cases this can cause worse trouble than already exists.

- **Injection Damp Proof Courses**

   Injection damp proof courses are not the universal answer to dampness. To work properly they need a horizontal layer or course of material which goes through the whole wall thickness to carry the liquid. Few stone walls have this and neither do stone plinths beneath timber frames.

   Injecting brick walls can work, as long as you are certain there is no timber in them. Injecting stone walls, particularly thick ones, rarely works and the pressure from the injection can push out the centre of the wall.

   It is very important that, if there is any timber in the wall, the damp proof course goes below the lowest piece of timber. Otherwise timber below the damp proof course will be subjected to an undue amount of wet and will rot.

   DO NOT LET ANYONE INJECT THE PANELS OF A TIMBER FRAMED BUILDING OR THE STRUCTURAL TIMBERS THEMSELVES.

Conclusion

Rising damp on its own is rarely a major cause of trouble. Usually very damp buildings are caused by directly penetrating water, either rain, leaking water pipes, forgotten wells or poor external drainage.

If your building is very wet, try to trace and cure the cause of the water first. Be systematic. Only move to inserting damp proof courses or waterproof coating as a last resort.

Keep the building well ventilated.

Chapter Nine

The Walls

Chapter Nine
The Walls

The most usual materials for walls of old buildings are earth, timber, stone and brick. The main cause of trouble in walls is water penetration, usually from leaky rainwater pipes, faulty drainage, or poorly maintained roof coverings. The second cause of trouble is later alterations and additions which have destroyed or affected the integrity of the structure.

The lack of what are today commonly called foundations is rarely in itself the cause of problems in an old building. Ground movement caused by excessive wetting or drying is often better taken up in a building without conventional foundations, because those buildings are designed to move with the seasons.

Earth

This is the oldest and originally, cheapest form of walling. It was used for the houses of the poor across the whole country, but now tends to survive in areas where other, less vulnerable materials were not available. Even in areas where other materials are used for houses and larger buildings you may find earth used for garden walls or outbuildings.

You may find earth walls being called cob or wichert or other local names. Whatever they are called, they are made of locally dug earth, with binding agents such as straw and mixed with water. The mixture is put in place in layers and beaten down. If earth walls get very wet, they simply fall apart, returning to the ground which they came from. Such walls must, therefore, be kept from direct contact with water.

Earth walls usually have roofs with overhanging eaves to throw water off and they are built on a base of whatever local stone is available. This is why earth garden walls have little roofs on them with overhanging edges. They are also given a coat of lime render or limewash.

Earth walls, if badly affected by water, can be difficult to repair. They can only be added to in height and even then making the new and old join together can be a problem. Additions and alterations are therefore not usually made to earth buildings in the same material.

It is also difficult to make openings in earth walls for windows and doors. The material cannot support its own weight over openings and consequently other materials such as timber or stone have to be used as lintels.

This means that windows and doors have to be small and that cutting new openings can, if not carefully done, cause the walls to collapse. So take the advice of a specialist before adding new openings or widening those existing.

Timber

Timber has been used for building from early times, for the whole structure of higher class buildings and for roofs on lesser buildings.

To make a structure from timber, you need to join the members together to form a frame and then to fill in the gaps with other materials, such as wattle and daub or brick.

The timbers are joined with traditional joints which are pegged with timber pegs.

- **Movement**

   These joints allow for the seasonal movement caused by changes in temperature and humidity. This must be expected in a structure made of organic materials. They should never be fixed so that they cannot move. If joints are rigidly fixed, then the seasonal movement must be taken up in other ways, for example, bending or splitting of the timbers themselves.

- **Foundations**

   Like earth walls, timber frames were built on low walls or plinths of whatever local stone was available in an attempt to reduce the effects of rising damp.

Alterations

Often timber frames will have been altered in the past. Parts of the frame may have been removed to make doorways or windows. The bottom members of a frame may have been replaced by brick or stone after they have rotted because of water penetration.

Such changes affect the stability of the structure which will have moved and settled to accommodate the re-distribution of stress.

Consequently, you need to be careful when making new alterations, for it is difficult, if not impossible, to predict what will happen.

- **Comprehensive Frame Survey**

  You may be asked for a comprehensive survey of a timber frame if you wish to do alterations or repairs. Without it the consequences of alterations will be very difficult to predict and could be disastrous.

- **Stripping**

  It should not be necessary to strip out later fabric of the building for such a survey.

  Excessive stripping can endanger the structure. The lathing which supports plaster can tie a weakened frame together and its removal can have unforeseen consequences.

Repair

If you think that your building may need repair, seek the advice of a local specialist. This may be the same person who has done your survey. Second opinions are also a good idea. A reputable specialist should not mind this, and may even welcome it.

Having gained advice and a survey, a reputable carpenter should be consulted. The specialist and carpenter should work together while the repairs are made. Any repairs should be minimal and done as far as possible by traditional methods of carpentry similar to those used on the existing building.

- **Timber for Repairs**

  All repairs to timber frames should be made in new timber, which should be of the same type as that being repaired, e.g. oak to oak, elm to elm etc.

  Green timber can be used. The drying out within the frame will add to the strength of the joints. In some cases it may help if the moisture content of the new is similar to that of the old. This must be done by the traditional method of air drying, not by drying the timber in a kiln.

  Avoid using secondhand timber or pegs. Pegs should be tapered and as dry as possible.

  Avoid the use of metal straps and plates as far as possible. Only use them where traditional timber repairs would result in removal of large areas of the old fabric. Metal fixings should be designed to allow for movement in the building.

Surface Treatment

Most timber frames need no surface treatment other than the occasional coat of limewash. Painting timber, brickwork, stone and render is a relatively modern fashion, which can seriously endanger the building by preventing the escape of moisture.

Surface treatment of timber framing with oils must be avoided. Linseed oil in particular attracts dirt and encourages insect attack.

Removal of existing paint can also damage structural timbers. If it is thought essential to remove paint, this must be done slowly and carefully, avoiding mechanical methods such as sandblasting, which removes the surface of the timber opening it up to attack by insects.

Where there has been insect attack and the timber surface has become powdery, only limited cleaning should take place. Defrassing or cleaning is often done with too much enthusiasm damaging the surface of timbers and destroying historical evidence of how the timber was worked.

If there is limited furniture beetle (woodworm) attack to main timbers don't worry too much, for these only eat the outer surface or sapwood. If the timbers have been properly produced in the traditional manner, then there will be a little sapwood on the edges, but mostly heartwood, which is only affected when it gets wet.

Infill Panels

These are the areas between the timbers of a frame. In earlier buildings they were filled with either woven twigs or wattles, or with cleft staves and laths. On top if this was daubed a mixture of earth and chopped straw or animal hair finished with coats of limewash or plastered with a lime plaster.

These panels are the same thickness as the timber framing and are soft enough to move with it.

As long as the outer surface is not broken and they do not get very wet, they can last for the life of the building. If they are broken or drilled, e.g. to get access for services in a roof space, then the wattle framework can be attacked by insects and consequently disintegrate.

During the 17th Century, bricks became more readily available and began to be used for infill in timber frames. Often during later centuries broken and decayed daub panels were replaced by bricks.

Existing infill panels whether brick or daub should only be removed as a last resort and like should be replaced with like.

Do not cover brick infill with render. Where this is done the render will stand proud of or may even be dressed over the timber, catching and holding water against it and causing decay.

Brick

Bricks are made from baked earth. They were a very expensive and fashionable material used mostly for large or prestigious buildings until the 17th Century. From around 1600 bricks began to be made more cheaply and in greater numbers. This meant that they could be used on lesser buildings. Thus bricks are found in chimneys on timber framed buildings and as infill for timber frames from that time onwards.

It took some time for complete walls of brick to be built, for the tradition of timber framing was so strong that even in brick buildings of the 18th Century, timber was often used in the brickwork behind the facing on external walls. A rough form of timber framing, without proper joints, surrounding brick panels was also used for internal walls. In this case laths were fixed over the framing to carry coats of plaster. The timber was never meant to be exposed and the laths gave stability to the wall. Such hidden timbers can be a menace if water enters the walls, for they can decay and weaken the brickwork without anyone realising that they are there.

As time went on, walls were constructed wholly of solid brickwork, until the end of the 19th Century when cavity walls began to be introduced.

- **Local Bricks**

   Earlier brickwork is concentrated in the localities where suitable clay could be found. Consequently the colour and texture of brickwork alters from place to place until the 19th Century when more mechanised brickworks were set up and railways and canals were used to transport bricks.

   Brickwork was also built in differing patterns known as bonds. These bonds depend on the date and type of building, but they are very important in defining the look of the walls.

- **Alterations**

   If you want to alter or extend your brick building you may be asked to match the bricks or the bond, so be prepared for this. It is very easy to destroy the character of a brick building by repairing with the wrong type of brickwork.

- **Joints and Mortar**

   Bricks are joined together with mortar. At first this was just another mix of mud, but gradual trial and error resulted in mixes of lime and sand being used.

   The idea is that the mortar joints should be weaker than the bricks so that any movement in the structure is taken up in the joints without the bricks themselves breaking. It is extremely important that any repair to brickwork uses a mortar mix which is similar to that existing.

   Most old mortars do not contain cement. This is a relatively new material. Bricks made by modern methods are usually harder than those made in the old way, so cement can be used in mortar for new buildings. When dealing with bricks made by the old methods cement should not be used in the mortar.

Repointing

Brickwork rarely needs repointing. Only if the mortar has been removed by some action, such as water running from a leaky rainwater pipe or running overflow, should repointing be considered. In this case the existing mortar mix and form of jointing should be copied. Repointing because the mortar seems soft is a waste of time and money. The mortar is meant to be soft.

With older, soft brickwork the use of hard mortars in repointing, especially if the mortar is brushed across the face of the brickwork or made to stand proud of it, will cause decay of the bricks by sealing in moisture which will then freeze in bad weather and push off the face of the bricks. Not only will you have wasted your money, but you may actually cause the building to collapse. So think carefully about repointing and only do it if absolutely necessary.

Excessive, incorrect or unnecessary repointing can alter the character and appearance of a building, cause damage to its structure and require Listed Building consent..

Stone

The type of stone use for building in any place depends on what is available in the locality. Thus the look of stone buildings varies from place to place. In areas where good building stone is not available other materials have been used for smaller buildings with stone being reserved only for the special or expensive buildings.

Worked or squared stone is expensive, so most walls are made of rough stone, called rubble with the dressed stone being saved for corners and around openings in walls.

The best dressed stone is called ashlar, being used as an outer facing to walls of more expensive buildings. It was quite common to render over rough stone and cut lines in the render to make it look like ashlar.

Construction

Stone walls are usually constructed of two outer skins of stone with the centre filled with rubble and mortar. In well built structures there will be occasional courses of stones which run through the whole thickness of the wall to tie the outer skins together. Do not rely on this being the case, particularly in small buildings or in areas where building stone is not readily available.

In some areas small stones such as flints are used for walls, these will need to have horizontal bands of stone or brick every so often in the wall to tie it together. Most stone walls therefore, cannot really be described as "solid". You will need to remember this and take care if you wish to make new window or door openings in them.

If the right precautions are not taken when making holes in stone walls you can lose the whole of the rubble filling leaving two slender, unstable skins of stone.

Joints, Mortar and Pointing

Like bricks, stones are held together with mortar. All the comments made earlier on mortar and pointing also relate to stone work. It is particularly important with pointing stonework to make sure that mortar is not brushed across the face of the stone, for this can hold in water causing the stone to crack and crumble.

Repair of stonework should always be done by a competent stonemason, it is not a job for the amateur.

External Wall Finishes

Brick and stone walls have their own natural finish and require nothing else on the outside of the building. Painting or adding other substances to them will alter their character and need Listed Building Consent. Timber frames must be able to breathe, painting them with impermeable oil based paints will cause them to rot. Timbers were traditionally left bare or painted with limewash.

Render

At some periods it was fashionable to cover the outside of stone or brick walls with a thick plaster finish called render. This was usually a soft material mixed from lime and sand. It is porous and allows the wall underneath to breathe.

While renders are sometimes painted they should not be treated with waterproof paints or substances for this will seal the wall causing decay and eventually the render will be pushed off by freezing water.

If render needs to be replaced, avoid strong mixes including cement, for these can be stronger than the base and seal in moisture. When this moisture freezes, it can push off the face of the wall structure along with the render.

If you are unfortunate enough to have a building which has a strong render coat, do not apply any other waterproofers for this will make matters worse. Taking this render off can also damage the building, for since it sticks very firmly to the base, attempts to remove it may also take off the surface of the wall.

Internal Wall Finishes

Inside buildings it has always been the practice to cover wall surfaces with some form of plaster, usually a mixture of lime, sand and chopped hair.

The idea of exposing brick or stone on the inside of a building is a later 20th Century fashion.

Stripping off old plaster may require Listed Building Consent and may, in some cases, endanger the structure of the building. Check before you do it.

Panelling

If people could afford it, they would line the inside of buildings with timber panelling. This would be over any plaster finish.

If your house is panelled, remember that most panelling was painted as were doors and staircases. The idea of cleaning off such paint is a late 20th Century fashion. Check before doing such work for you may destroy part of the history of your building by removing early paint covered by layers of later paint.

Wall and Ceiling Paintings

In other cases the plaster and timber framing may have been covered with paintings of scenes, quotations, symbols and decorative patterns. This sort of painting was also done on ceilings.

If such paintings are discovered you will need to have the advice of a specialist before anything is done to them. Removal of such paintings would be an offence.

External and Internal Repainting

For repainting, it is best to use permeable paints of the older, water or oil based types, or limewash. These are now available from specialist suppliers.

Foundations

Few early buildings have what we today would call foundations.

This is nothing to worry about. If the buildings have survived several hundred years without foundations they should go on for many more if they are not interfered with.

Problems can happen when ground conditions change, e.g. very dry summers or extra water from overflowing drains. Such things are less likely to affect old buildings than new ones, for the old structures are built to take up movement.

Sometimes later additions to old buildings cause trouble if they are linked firmly to the old structure. The new part on its modern foundations will stand still, while the old part will want to flex and move with the seasons, consequently, any undue movement will be taken up in the old building rather than the new. Beware of this if you decide to have an extension built. Underpinning only part of an old building can have the same effect.

Chapter Ten

Doors, Windows
and Fireplaces

Chapter Ten
Doors, Windows and Fireplaces.

The Importance of Detail

While the structure of the building is important, smaller details are also essential to its character. This includes windows, doors, fireplaces, plasterwork, staircases and other details, all of which combine to create the character of the building.

It is therefore important to be aware of these things and take care of them along with the rest of the building. You will need Listed Building Consent to change them. Remember that much of the atmosphere of an old house lies in the patina of age. By removing such details you can loose this for ever. Try to be aware of what details you have in the building and be sympathetic to them if you are forced to replace or repair. Most of these details started off as simply practical needs. The way they look and are made comes from the practical need for making items from the materials available. To cover an opening in a wall, when the most easily used material was timber, meant that several smaller pieces of wood had to be joined to make a flat panel for a door. For a window, small pieces of glass had to be joined into a panel with lead strips or wooden bars.

The way old doors and windows are made is as much a record of the stages of past knowledge as is the way the whole building is constructed. There was a gradual development over the centuries, which it is important to notice and preserve. Today doors and windows can be made with different methods and materials from those of the past. The details such as panels in doors or glazing bars in windows are not necessary for their construction. Doors and windows made by the new methods to look like the old do not, and cannot, look right. This is why the replacement of old doors and windows is often resisted by those who administer the Listed Building laws.

New materials and methods are not bad. They simply need to be understood and used honestly, with care for the balance between old and new. If there had been no changes in the past, we would not have the variety of buildings which survive today.

Doors

Early doors were made of wooden boards. The most expensive had two layers of boards at right angles to each other, nailed together with as many nails as could be afforded. Because sawn boards and nails were expensive, less expensive doors had one layer of board held together with two or three pieces of wood called ledges nailed across them. This kind of door, known as "ledged and battened", was made throughout the centuries as the cheapest door available until this century, when new ways of manufacturing produced the "flush" door. Even when panelled doors came into more general use in the 1700s, ledged and battened doors were used on lesser buildings and rooms such as outhouses and kitchens.

Internal doors did not need to be as strong as external doors and lighter forms of doors made of thin panels in wooden frames evolved from the panelling used to line the walls of rooms. External doors had to be strong and it took a little time for panelled doors to be used outside. They needed to have panels small enough and frames thick enough to deter intruders. During the 1700s, two panelled doors were often used inside buildings, with six panelled doors being made for outside use. Six panelled doors were more expensive to make, and are less likely to be found on simple buildings, but may be found inside and out of grand buildings. By the 1800s, four panelled doors were being used inside and outside.

- **Hierarchy of Doors**

   Most buildings have a hierarchy of doors. The more expensive doors were used on the better rooms, with the best faces towards the more important spaces, and cheaper doors for lesser rooms. In considering the character of your building you need to be aware of this. Replacing all the doors with the same type can take away this record of the past use of the building. Try to keep what doors you have. Even if they are damaged, a good joiner can repair them in the traditional manner. Remember that, apart from the early boarded doors, doors have always been painted, and the idea of exposing the bare wood is a recent fashion.

Door & Window Fittings

Hinges, locks and handles on both doors and windows, are worth noticing and keeping. They also evolved over the years and can give you an insight into building's past use. Locks were the property of the tenant and so were taken away with them. This is why some doors have several keyholes.

Windows

Before the late 1500s most buildings did not have glass in their windows. It was an expensive, imported luxury. Windows were covered by wooden shutters made like the early doors. The glass which began to be made in Britain after that time could only be produced in small pieces, which had to be joined together with lead strips and fixed into wooden or iron frames. Opening lights were hinged, like doors, at the sides. Hinged windows are called casements.

Lead reacts to changes in temperature by expanding and contracting. Eventually it loses its elasticity causing the leaded lights to sag. When this happens the window can be taken apart, the lead melted down and the glass re-set. Because of this need for re-leading, not many really early leaded lights survive, and over the years much early glass has also been lost.

If you have leaded lights which need repair, try to make sure you use an experienced craftsman and that any old glass is re-used. Your Local Authority Conservation Officer should be able to advise you on local craftsmen, and you might even be able to get a grant.

Sash Windows

Around 1700 a new type of window was introduced into this country, called a sash window. Sash windows slide. Some slide vertically and others horizontally. Horizontal sliding sashes are sometimes called Yorkshire sashes.

The sash window became very fashionable. In many existing buildings, the old leaded casements were replaced by sashes. If people could not afford to put sashes in all their windows, they would put them in the most important rooms.

You may have a hierarchy of windows in your building, with sashes at the front and casements at the back. If this is the case, it would destroy both the history and the character of the building to replace them all with one kind of window.

Glazing Bars

In sash windows the sheets of glass were joined together by wooden glazing bars. Early glazing bars are quite thick, but, as time went on, they were made thinner to give the impression that the window had only one sheet of glass.

Even casements began to be made from wooden frames with glazing bars. The thickness and detail of glazing bars plays a significant part in the look of the window. If you are forced to replace a window completely, make sure that not only the type of window, but the size and detail of the glazing bars is copied.

Glass

The ways of making early glass could only produce relatively small panes. These were often discoloured and varying in thickness. The first glass for windows was made by blowing a bubble, cutting off the two ends to form a cylinder and then cutting down one long side and flattening it out. This is called cylinder glass.

The second way of making glass was to blow a bubble, cut off one end and spin the glass until it formed a disc. This is called crown glass. The centre of the disc called the bullion, was thick and bulbous. This was the cheapest piece of glass. The disc got thinner towards the edge and had spiral marks across it caused by the spinning. These marks can easily be seen in window panes made of crown glass.

If you have early glass in your windows try to keep it, for such glass is hard to replace. Over the years, people aimed at windows which were as near as possible to single, clear sheets of glass. They even took glazing bars out of existing windows, when large sheets of glass became available.

The present fashion for small paned windows is out of step with this trend and has resulted in the production of large sheets of glass with fake glazing bars or leading. This type of glazing can never fit in with the early windows. Its use in a Listed Building would need consent and would be unlikely to receive it.

Double Glazing

Many early buildings had shutters as well as windows. Shutters gave security as well as cutting down draughts during the night. If you have shutters, why not try using them. Most old windows are not capable of direct double glazing without destroying their form and character, but some can be draught proofed.

If you want to go further than draught proofing, you could try secondary windows fixed inside the old ones. You must consider the design of these carefully. Rigid metal frames and large sheets of glass will not allow for the natural movement of an old building in the same way as the older forms of window will. If they are used they may cause unnecessary concern by bending and buckling.

Beware when sealing a building, for without ventilation, water vapour in the air can condense in unexpected places causing rot. It is also wise to remember that open fires need air. Sealing windows and doors against draughts will either stop the fires burning or make them smoke.

Fireplaces

In very early houses the main room was open to the roof and heated by a fire on an open hearth in the middle of the room and without a chimney. This is how some old roofs became covered with soot.

Chimneys were first put into large houses and only in small houses from around 1550 onwards. In some poor houses it took until this century for the central hearth to be replaced by a chimney. The early fireplaces and chimneys were experimental. It took until the early 1800s for a set of rules to be made for a reliable fireplace.

If you have an old house you must not expect every fireplace to be large. Only the cooking fireplaces needed to be big. In other cases the fireplace would be as small as could be built depending on the size of the room. This is to cut down the intake of air and avoid smoking.

Surrounds

From the beginning if could be afforded, the fireplace has a surround of wood, plaster, stone etc. In buildings constructed after 1700 you must expect this for every fireplace.

Later it was popular to fill in the opening within these surrounds to bring it down to the best size for a good fire. Taking out this filling and removing later grates not only needs Listed Building Consent, but can also leave you with a fireplace which doesn't work properly. It can even cause the chimney to collapse.

The fact that there is an arch above the fireplace in a brick or stone chimney does not necessarily mean that this was the extent of the fireplace. Such arches were often used to take some of the weight off flat timber lintels.

If you want to investigate blocked fireplaces, check with the Local Authority first, for you will probably need Listed Building Consent and the Local Authority conservation staff may be able to advise you. Think carefully about it before you start work. Tap the wall to find any hollow places. Drill some experimental holes first. You may need to support the upper floor while doing such work.

Other Details

Here is a note of some of the other details you may need to be aware of:-

> Staircases; ornamental plasterwork; wrought iron work; early wallpaper; panelling; built-in cupboards (often from 1600s and 1700s); mirrors, statues etc if they are fixtures and a part of the overall design of the building; floors, e.g. very old boarding, painted floors, plaster floors; porches, hoods, canopies and doorcases.

General Conclusions

*   Be aware of your buildings as a moving, breathing structure in its own right.

*   Do minor repairs and maintenance as soon as you find they are needed.

*   Think carefully and get advice before doing major repairs.

*   If you need advice look for a local specialist rather than a national "name".

*   Use tried and tested methods. Beware of short cuts. They can cause more problems than they solve.

*   As far as possible replace like with like.

*   Be prepared to put up with the occasional draught and a small amount of dampness. Nothing is perfect!

*   Keep gutters clear and rainwater goods in order.

*   Remember buildings are made of combinations of materials which each move in their own way with the seasons. Consequently, you will not stop water coming in somewhere, so give it the chance of escaping by evaporation. That is, do not fully seal any part of the structure with so called waterproof materials.

*   Always keep the building well ventilated, especially small enclosed spaces.

*   If you are unsure of what to do and what needs Listed Building Consent ask your Local Authority for advice.

*   Most of all, enjoy your building and all the quirks which go to make up its character.

Glossary

ABUTMENT	Junction between roof of one building and wall of higher building.
ANCIENT MONUMENT	A building or area of land entered in the Schedule of Ancient Monuments prepared under the Ancient Monuments and Archaeological Areas Act, 1970. See page 10.
BEAM	A horizontal structural timber.
BOROUGH COUNCIL	Local Authority, third tier of Government, after Parliament and County Councils.
BUILDING PRESERVATION NOTICE	See page 3.
CASEMENTS	Hinged windows.
CHASE	A groove cut in structure of building to take a pipe etc.
CLEFT	Split. Where a piece of timber has been split along its length with wedges, axes etc rather than sawn.
CONSERVATION OFFICER	Local Authority Officer dealing particularly with Listed Buildings and Conservation, usually a specialist in this field.
CROWN GLASS	Spun glass. See page 55 & 56.
CYLINDER GLASS	See page 55.

DEFRASSING	Cleaning off debris left on timber by wood boring insects.
DETAILS	Large scale drawings of parts of a building.
DISTRICT COUNCIL	Local Authority, third tier of Government, after Parliament and County Councils.
ELEVATION	Drawing of facade or side of building.
LISTED BUILDING ENFORCEMENT NOTICE	See page 9.
ENGLISH HERITAGE	Popular name of Historic Buildings and Monuments Commission for England. A body set up and funded by Government to give advice to the Secretaries of State, Local Authorities and the public on ancient monuments, historic buildings and conservation areas.
FILLET	A strip of mortar or cement laid across the junction between a roof and a wall or chimney at an abutment
FLASHING	A piece of sheet material, usually lead, laid across the junction between a roof and wall or chimney at an abutment (see above).
GLAZING BARS	Thin pieces of wood which supports panes of glass within a timber window frame.
GULLEY	A receptacle for the collection of water at the end of a drain, usually with a grating over the top.
HISTORICAL BUILDINGS AND MONUMENTS COMMISSION FOR ENGLAND	See English Heritage.
JOISTS	Horizontal structural timbers which support floors.
LATHS	Thin strips of wood used for supporting roof coverings or plaster.
LEDGED AND BATTENED DOOR	A door constructed of vertical boards, called battens, nailed on to horizontal pieces of timber called ledges.

LIMEWASH	A mixture of lime, water and other substances e.g. tallow, used as a finish to walls, ceiling etc. The traditional wall finish which allows the building structure to "breathe".
LINTEL	A horizontal member placed across an opening in a wall to support the load of the wall above the opening.
LOCAL AUTHORITY	Local arm of Government, usually District or Borough Council.
LONG STRAW	A method of thatching using corn straw, where the straws are not lined up with butt ends together.
PARAPET	A wall at the top of a building which projects above the lowest point of the roof.
PITCH	Slope of roof.
PLAN	Drawing showing floor of building.
PLANNING COMMITTEE	Group of elected Local Councillors who consider and decide on planning applications.
PLANNING OFFICER	Local Authority Officer dealing with planning matters.
PLANNING POLICY GUIDANCE NOTE	A document issued by the Government to give further explanation of the thinking behind the planning laws. Often used by Local Authority staff and Planning Inspectors when dealing with appeals.
PLUMBER	A specialist working in lead.
PROUD	Used to describe part of a building which stands forward from the rest of the building.
PUBLIC INQUIRY	See page 21.
LISTED BUILDING PURCHASE NOTICE	See page 10.
RAFTER	An inclined timber which supports the roof covering.
REPAIRS NOTICE	See page 24.

RENDER	Thick coat of plaster type wall covering.
RIDGE	Top of roof, junction of two slopes.
SASH	A sliding window.
SECTION	Drawing showing vertical slice of building.
SCHEDULE OF ANCIENT MONUMENTS	A list of buildings and sites drawn up under the Ancient Monuments and Archaeological Areas Act 1970. See page 10.
STAVE	Vertical piece of timber, usually cleft, used to form support for daub panels in some timber frames.
THATCH	Covering roofs with vegetable material. Word derives from saxon name for roof covering.
TIMBER FRAME	The main structure of a building which is formed from timber members jointed together with traditional carpentry joints.
TIE BEAM	A horizontal timber fixed between the feet of two rafters to resist the outward thrust of the weight of the roof covering.
WATER REED	A material used for thatching. It grows mostly in Norfolk, Dorset and the coastal areas of Wales. Thus it is the local roof covering for buildings in those areas.
WATTLE & DAUB	A method of filling the spaces between the timbers of a structural frame, consisting of a mixture of earth, water and chopped straw or hair plastered onto a frame of woven sticks or staves and laths.

Extract from
Archaeological Survey

(All plans have been reduced from a larger scale)

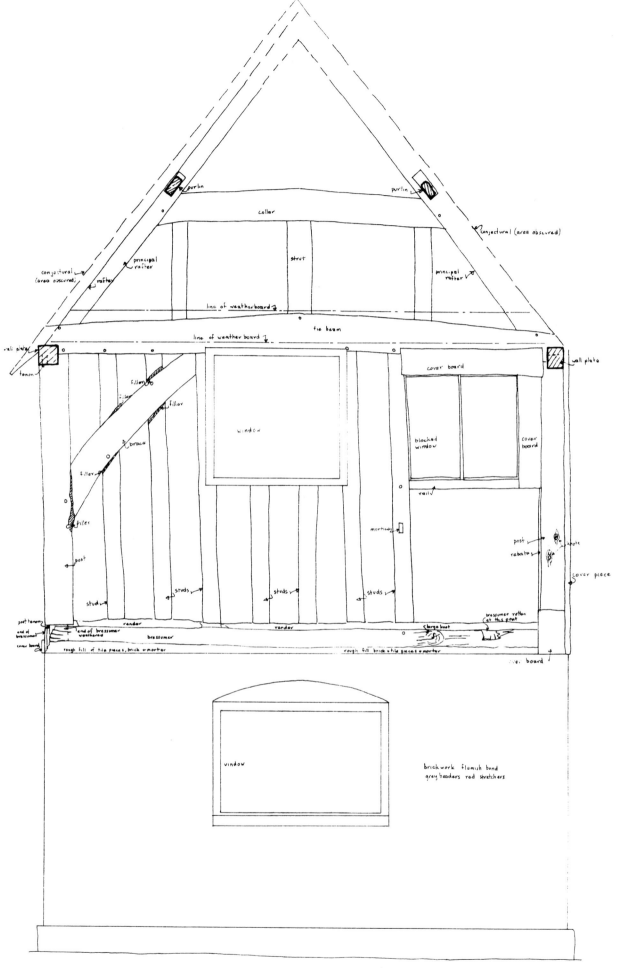

purlin

purlin

collar

conjectural (area obscured)

principal rafter

strut

principal rafter

conjectural (area obscured)

rafter

line of weatherboard

line of weather board

tie beam

wall plate

cover board

wall plate

tenon

filler

window

blocked window

cover board

filler

filler

brace

rail

filler

mortices

filler

post

rebate

knots

post

cover piece

studs

studs

studs

stud

post tenon

render

render

bressumer rotten (at this point)

end of bressumer

end of bressumer weathered

bressumer

large knot

cover board

rough fill of tile pieces, brick + morter

rough fill brick + tile pieces + morter

cover board

window

brickwork flemish bond
grey headers red stretchers

West Elevation

**Newchurch Cottage
Hafod
Fullbridge
Oxford**

Measured & Drawn by
Josephine M. Cormier   May 1993

0   ½   1 metre

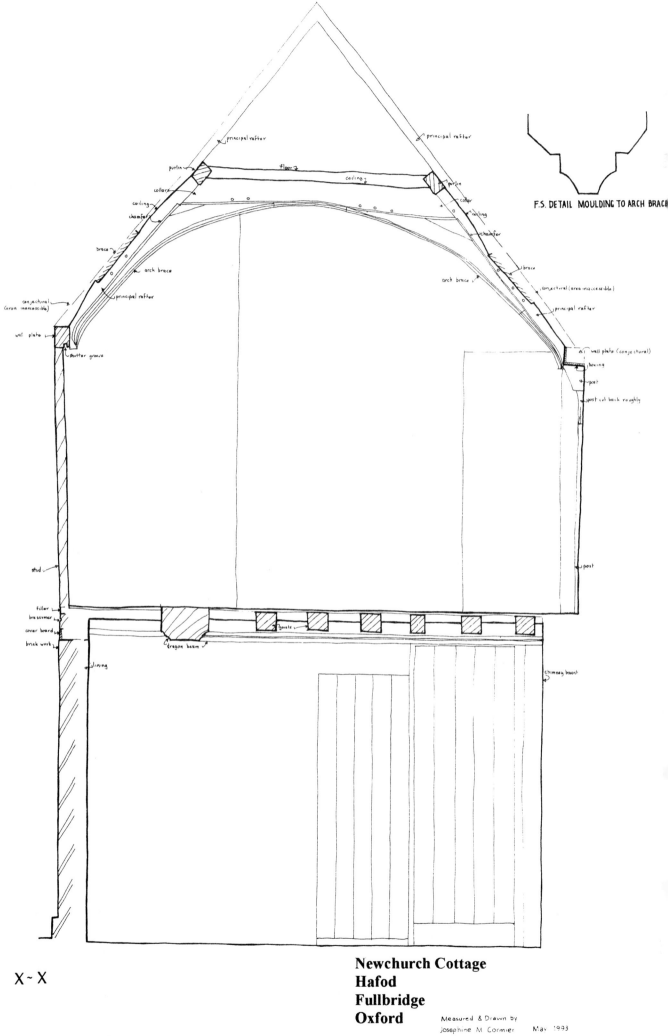

F.S. DETAIL MOULDING TO ARCH BRACE

principal rafter
principal rafter
purlin
floor?
ceiling
purlin
collar
collar
ceiling
ceiling
chamfer
chamfer
brace
arch brace
arch brace
brace
conjectural (area inaccessible)
conjectural (area inaccessible)
principal rafter
principal rafter
wall plate
wall plate (conjectural)
shutter groove
boxing
post
post cut back roughly
stud
post
filler
bressumer
cover board
joists
brick work
dragon beam
lining
chimney breast

X ~ X

Newchurch Cottage
Hafod
Fullbridge
Oxford

Measured & Drawn by
Josephine M. Cormier   May 1993

0   ½   1 metre

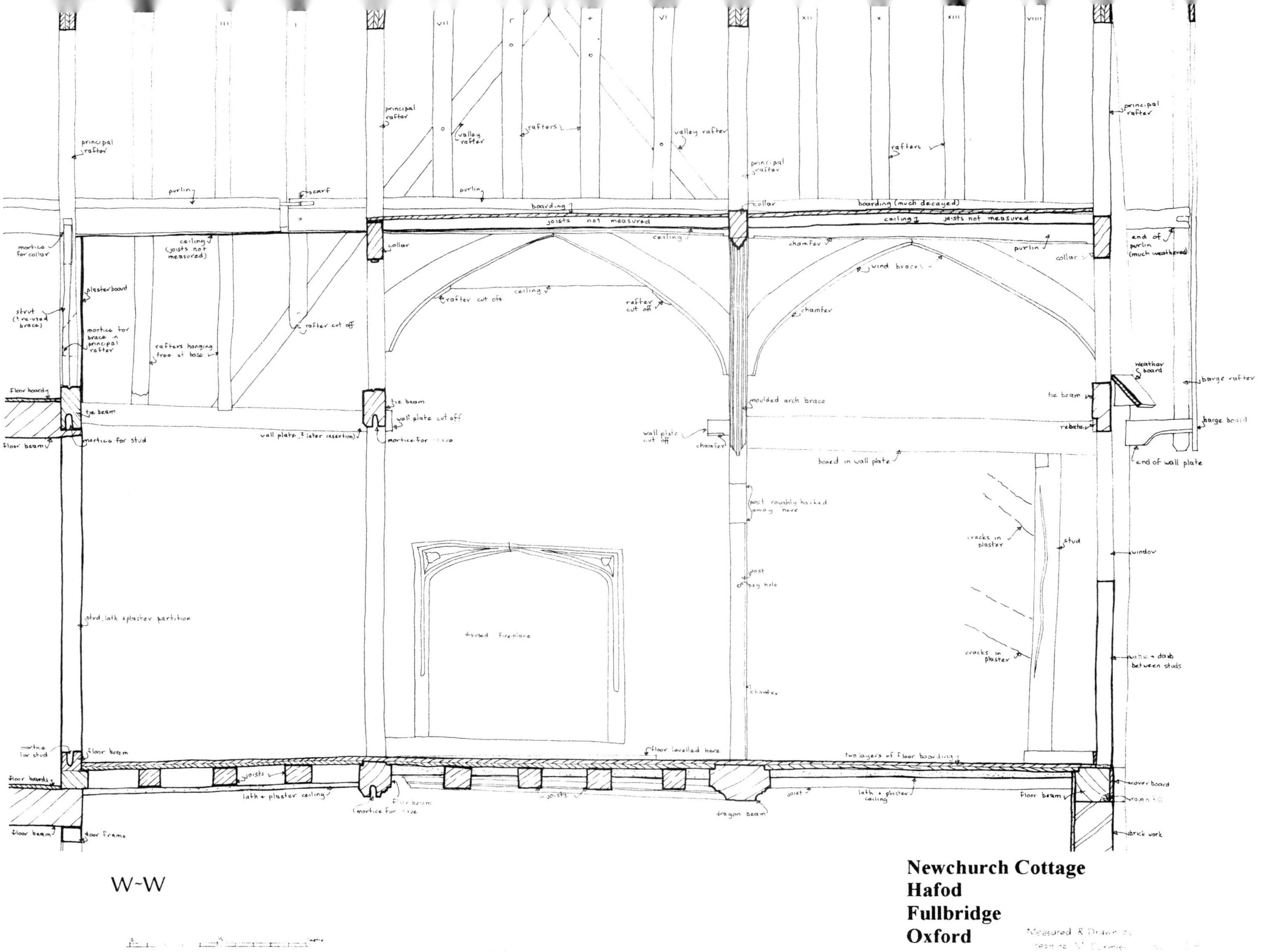

Newchurch Cottage
Hafod
Fullbridge
Oxford

Measured & Drawn by

W-W

principal rafter

barge rafter
barge board
end of purlin (much weathered)
weather board
end of wall plate
window
wattle daub between studs
cover board
crown tile
brick work
floor beam

tie beam
rebate
stud
cracks in plaster
cracks in plaster

rafters
boarding (much decayed)
ceiling 1
joists not measured
purlin
collar
wind braces
chamfer
chamfer
moulded arch brace
board in wall plate
lath + plaster ceiling
two layers of floor boarding

principal rafter
collar
ceiling
joists not measured
boarding
wall plate cut off
rafter cut off
chamfer
(most roughly hacked away here)
peg hole
joist
chamfer
dragon beam
floor levelled here

valley rafter

rafters
valley rafter
purlin
joists
rafter cut off
ceiling 3
rafter cut off
tie beam
wall plate cut off
mortice for brace
wall plate: later insertion
disused fireplace
joists
lath + plaster ceiling
floor beam
mortice for brace

principal rafter
collar
scarf
rafter cut off
purlin
ceiling joists not measured
plasterboard
mortice for brace on principal rafter
rafters hanging free at base
old lath & plaster partition
tie beam
mortice for stud
floor beam
joists
lath + plaster ceiling
floor beam
mortice for stud
floor boards
door frame

principal rafter
mortice for collar
strut (raised brace)
floor boarding
floor beam

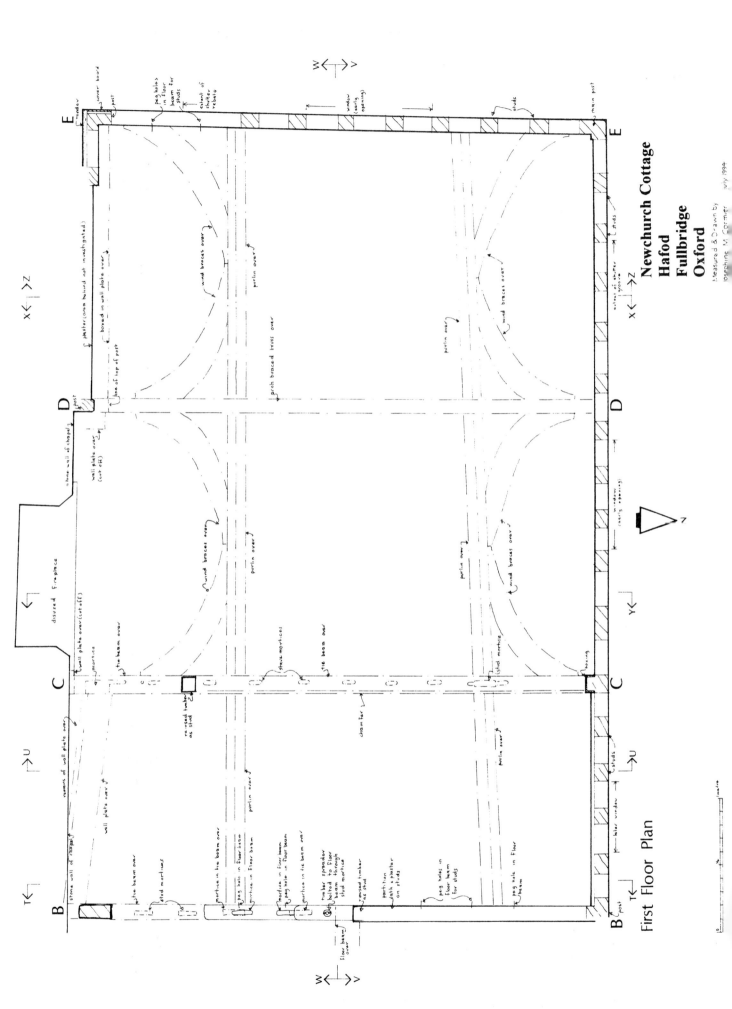

First Floor Plan

Newchurch Cottage
Hafod
Fullbridge
Oxford

Measured & Drawn by
Josephine M. Cormier   July 1994

Model Application
Form and Plans

As Existing

- Ground Floor Plan
- First Floor Plan
- North Elevation
- West, East and South Elevations

As Proposed

- Ground Floor Plan
- First Floor Plan
- North Elevation
- East and South Elevations
- Site Location and Window Details
- Replacement Stair Details

(All plans have been reduced from a larger scale)

OLDTOWN DISTRICT COUNCIL
LISTED BUILDING CONSENT APPLICATION
APPLICATION FOR CONSENT TO CARRY OUT WORKS TO
A LISTED BUILDING UNDER THE TOWN AND COUNTRY PLANNING ACTS

Please answer ALL QUESTIONS in BLOCK LETTERS. If a question is not applicable, answer N/A in space. Please send FOUR copies of this form and supporting plans, drawings and photographs to:

FOR OFFICE USE ONLY

THE DIRECTOR OF PLANNING SERVICES,
OLD TOWN DISTRICT COUNCIL,
COUNCIL OFFICES, MARKET STREET,
OLDTOWN, PR12 2OL
Tel: Oldtown 15889

1.		APPLICANT S NAME	L. B. OWNER
		ADDRESS	MARET HOUSE EDDIES HILL FULLBRIDGE
		POSTCODE	P R 11 3AN PHONE FULLBRIDGE 63091
2.	If the applicant has an agent, all correspondence will be sent to the Agent.	AGENTS NAME	A. GENT
		ADDRESS	THE STUDIO FAIRFIELD ROAD OLDTOWN PI2 1DL
		CONTACT NAME	A. GENT PHONE OLDTOWN 61249
3.	(a) The site of the Application Building must be shown EDGED RED on the submitted plans. Any other land controlled by the applicant to be EDGED BLUE.	BUILDING LOCATION	NEWCHURCH COTTAGE HAFOD FULLBRIDGE
	(b) What is the existing use of the building. if vacant, state this together with last use of building.	BUILDING USE	DWELLING HOUSE
	(c) State the grading of the building in the list of Buildings of Special Architectural or Historical Interest	LISTED GRADE	II
4.	WHAT IS THE APPLICATION FOR? Give brief details of the proposed works both internal and External.		DEMOLITION OF SHED REMOVAL OF PARTITION AND STAIR AND BATHROOM. PROVISION OF NEW BATHROOM, STAIR, REPLACEMENT OF WINDOW AND PART OF EXTERNAL WALL.
5.	Please list all plans, drawings and photographs submitted with application.	PLANS/ DRAWINGS	AS EXISTING:• GROUND FLOOR PLAN •FIRST FLOOR PLAN •NORTH ELEVATION •WEST, EAST + SOUTH EL. AS PROPOSED:• GROUND FLOOR PLAN • FIRST FLOOR PLAN • NORTH ELEVATION • EAST + SOUTH ELEVATIONS • SITE LOCATION + WINDOW DETAILS • REPLACEMENT STAIR DETAILS
6.	State the applicant's interest in the land. E.g. Owner, lessee, potential purchaser.	OWNERSHIP	OWNER
7.	Are there any prposals for a new building on the site? Give brief details and any related planning application number.		NO

SIGNED: A. Gent .... ON BEHALF OF: L.B. OWNER .... DATE: 11.02.95

Before submitting the application check that it is complete, that all questions have been answered, and the form signed.

UNDER REGULATION 6 OF THE TOWN AND COUNTRY PLANNING (LISTED BUILDINGS AND BUILDINGS IN CONSERVATION AREAS) REGULATIONS 1987

I hereby certify that:

1. No person other than the applicant was an owner of any part of the land to which the application relates at the beginning of the period of 20 days before the date of the accompanying application.

2. None of the land to which the application relates constitutes or forms part of an agricultural holding.

Signed: *a. gent*   Date: 11.02.95

on behalf of: L.B. OWNER

UNDER REGULATION 6 OF THE TOWN AND COUNTRY PLANNING (LISTED BUILDINGS AND BUILDINGS IN CONSERVATION AREAS) REGULATIONS 1987

I hereby certify that:

1. The requisite Notice No. 1 has been given to the owner(s) of the land to which the application relates at the beginning of twenty days before the date of accompanying application.

    Name and address of owner: ....

    ....

    Date of Service of Notice No. 1: ....

2. None of the land to which the application relates constitutes or forms part of an agricultural holding.

Signed: .... Date: ....

on behalf of: ....

UNDER REGULATION 6 OF THE TOWN AND COUNTRY PLANNING (LISTED BUILDINGS AND BUILDINGS IN CONSERVATION AREAS) REGULATIONS 1987

An application for planning permission is being made to Newbury District Council and you are owner/part owner of the application site.

Address of application site: ....

....

Description of proposal: ....

Name and address of applicant: ....

....

If you wish to make representations on this proposal, please do so within three weeks of receiving this notice to the Director of Planning Services, Newbury District Council, Council Offices, Market St., Newbury, Berks.

Signed: .... Date: ....

on behalf of: ....

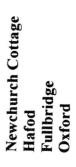

Ground Floor Plan

**Newchurch Cottage
Hafod
Fullbridge
Oxford**

Measured & Drawn by
Josephine M. Cormier   May 1993

E

D

C

B

A

SHED

W.C.

KITCHEN

LOBBY

SITTING ROOM

fireplace

fireplace

cupboard

line of beam over

line of joist over

door closed off

line of wagon beam over

line of joist over

Area closed off and available for inspection

E

D

C

B

A

X

Y

Z

N

1 metre

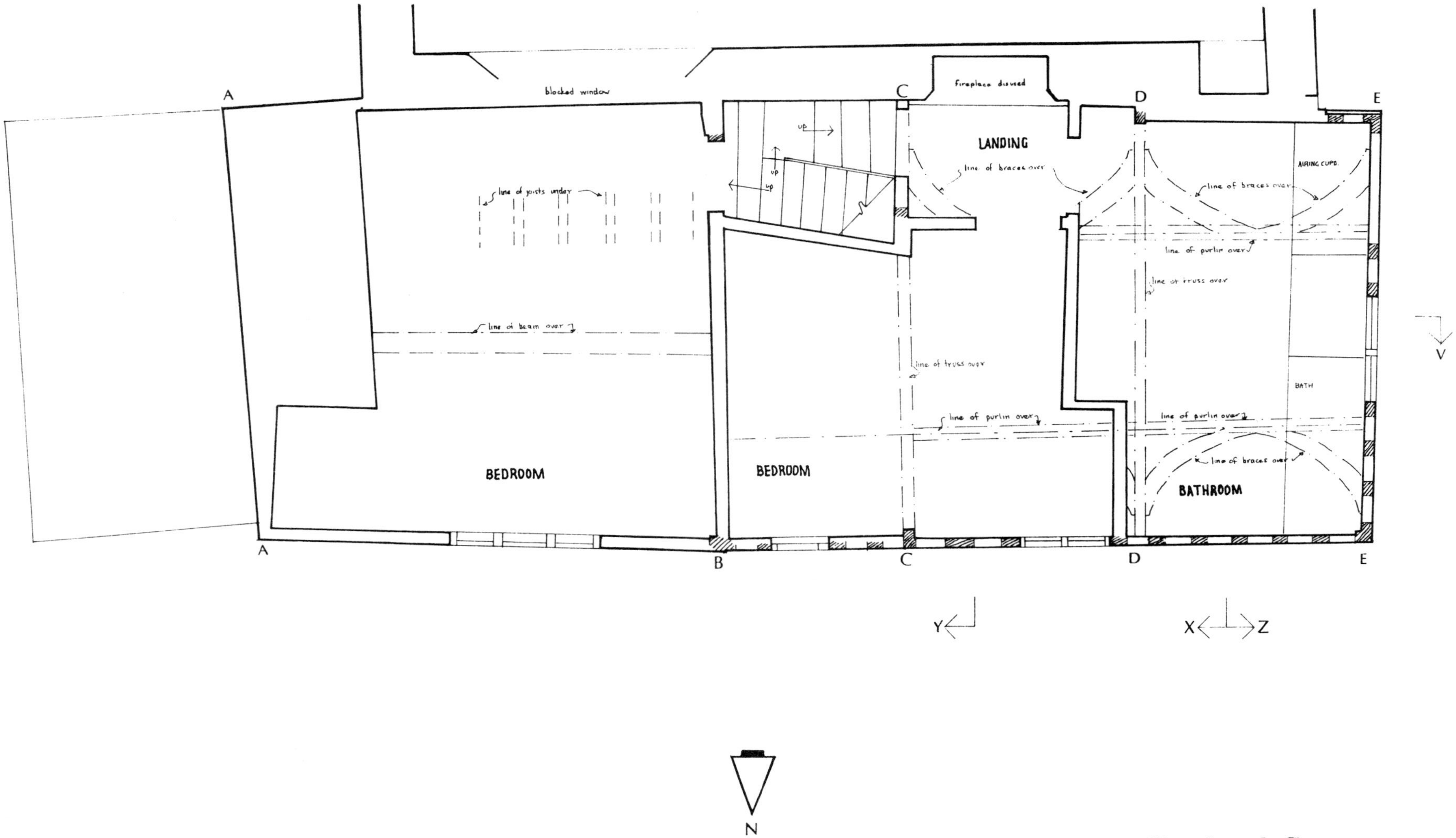

First Floor Plan

Newchurch Cottage
Hafod
Fullbridge
Oxford

Measured & Drawn by
Josephine M. Cormier   May 1993

BEDROOM

BEDROOM

BATHROOM

LANDING

AIRING CUPD

BATH

Fireplace disused

blocked window

line of joists under

line of beam over

line of braces over

line of purlin over

line of truss over

line of purlin over

line of braces over

line of purlin over

line of truss over

line of purlin over

line of braces over

up

N

North Elevation

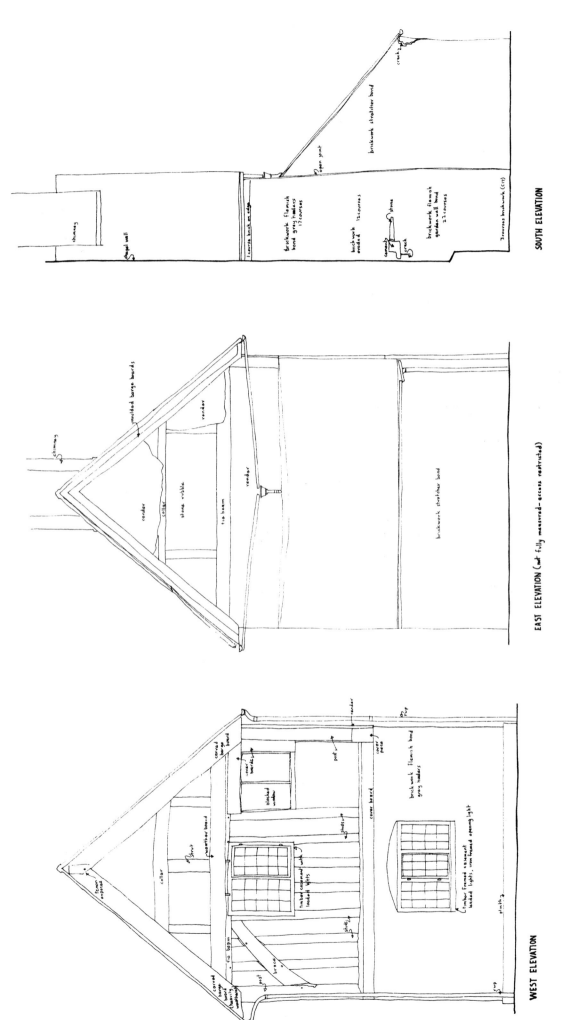

SOUTH ELEVATION

EAST ELEVATION (not fully measured - access restricted)

WEST ELEVATION

Newchurch Cottage
Hafod
Fullbridge
Oxford

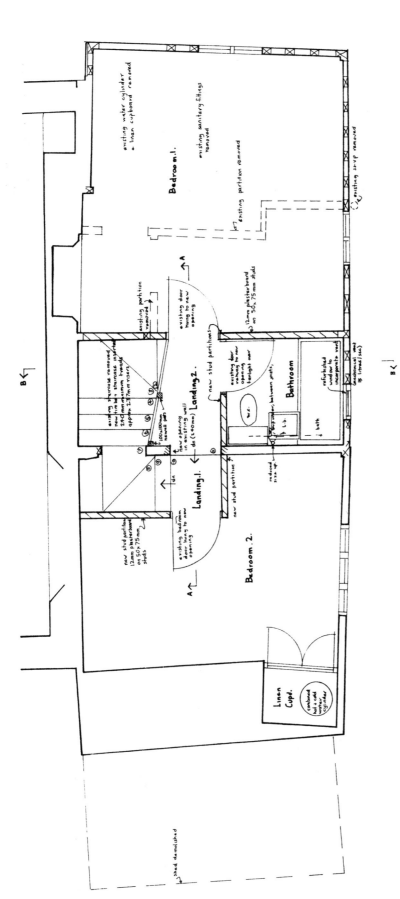

First Floor Plan

Scale 1:20

N

Newchurch Cottage
Hafod
Fullbridge
Oxford

PROPOSED ALTERATIONS

Drawn by Josephine M. Cormier   August 1993

1

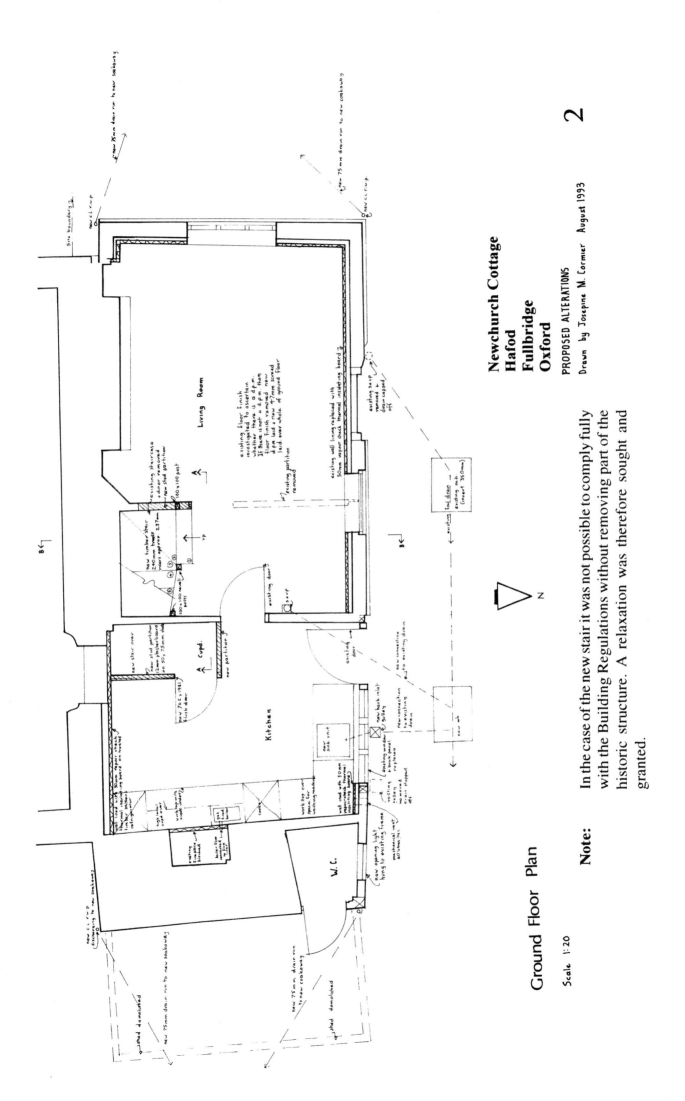

Ground Floor Plan

Scale 1:20

Newchurch Cottage
Hafod
Fullbridge
Oxford

PROPOSED ALTERATIONS

Drawn by Josephine M. Cormier   August 1993

2

Note: In the case of the new stair it was not possible to comply fully with the Building Regulations without removing part of the historic structure. A relaxation was therefore sought and granted.

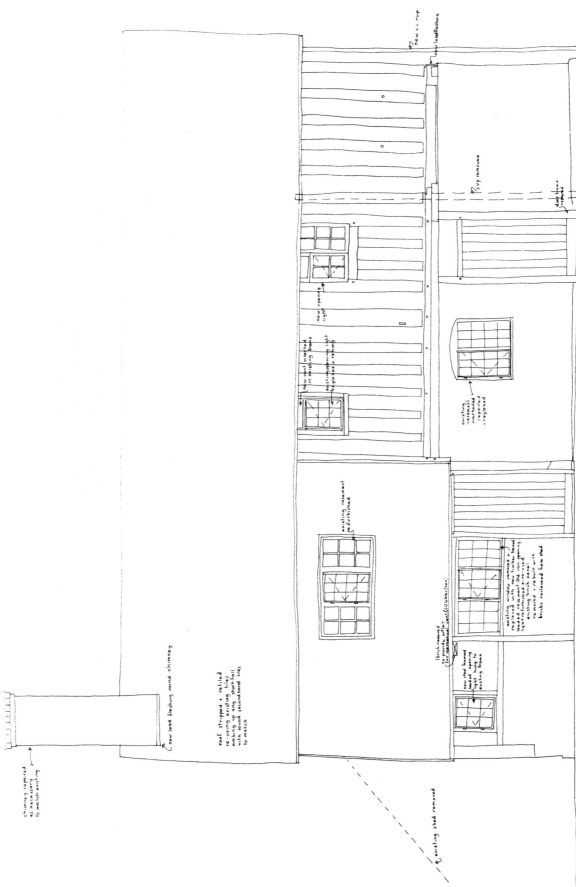

North Elevation

Scale 1:20

Newchurch Cottage
Hafod
Fullbridge
Oxford

PROPOSED ALTERATIONS

Drawn by Josephine M. Lorimer August 1993

3

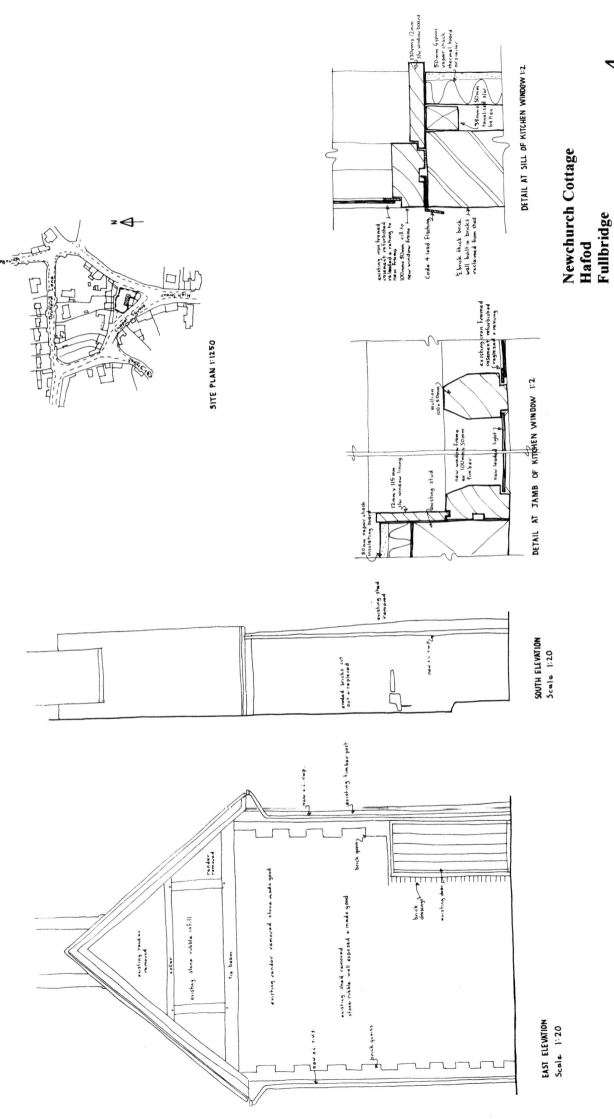

DETAIL AT SILL OF KITCHEN WINDOW 1:2

DETAIL AT JAMB OF KITCHEN WINDOW 1:2

SITE PLAN 1:1250

SOUTH ELEVATION
Scale 1:20

EAST ELEVATION
Scale 1:20

Newchurch Cottage
Hafod
Fullbridge
Oxford

PROPOSED ALTERATIONS

Drawn by Josephine M. Cormier August 1993

4

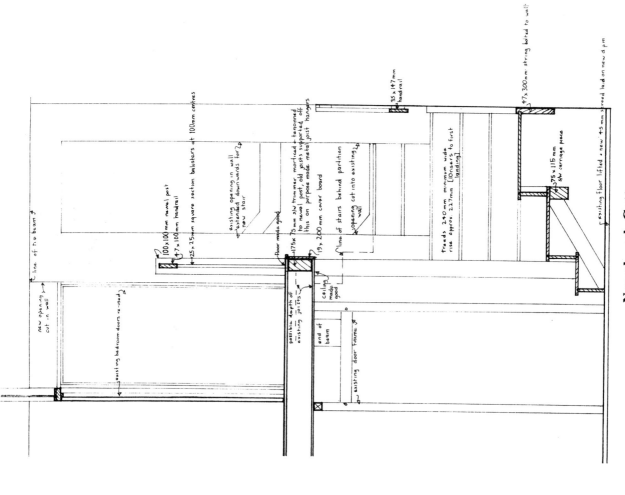

B~B

Newchurch Cottage
Hafod
Fullbridge
Oxford
PROPOSED ALTERATIONS

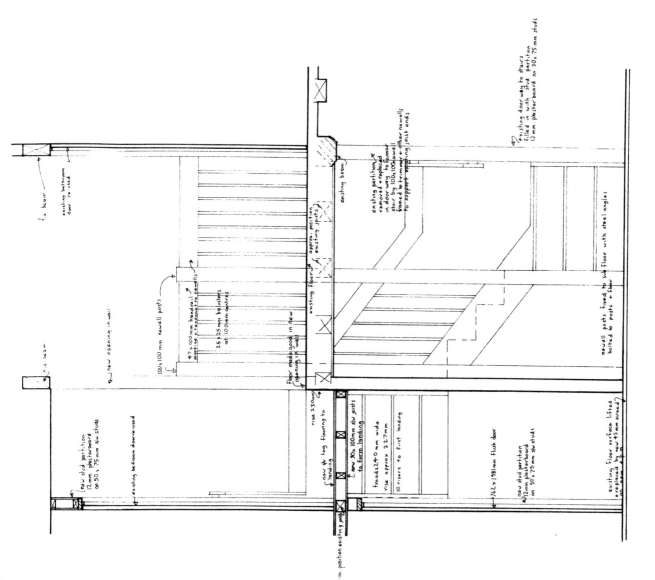

A~A

Scale 1:10

Addresses

Ancient Monuments Society	St Ann's Vestry Hall 2 Church Entry London, EC4V 5HB 0171 236 3934
Department of National Heritage	2-4 Cockspur Street London, SW1Y 5DH 0171 211 6000
Department of the Environment	2 Marsham Street London, SW1P 3EB 0171 973 3000
English Heritage	Fortress House 23 Savile Row London, W1X 1AB 0171 973 3000
The Council for British Archaeology	Bowes Morrell House 111 Walmgate York, YO1 2UV 01904 671417
The Georgian Group	37 Spital Square London, E1 6DY 0171 377 1722

Addresses

The Royal Commission on the Historical
Monuments of England

Fortress House
23 Savile Row
London, W1X 1AB

0171 973 3500

Alexander House
19 Fleming Way
Swindon
SN8 2NG

01793 414100

Shelley House
Acomb Road
York, YO2 4HB

01904 784411

The Society for the Protection of Ancient
Buildings

37 Spital Square
London, E1 6DY

0171 377 1644

The Victorian Society

1 Priory Gardens
Bedford Park
London, W4 1TT

0181 944 1019

Titles of Interest

Book

Order

Form

PLANNING PERMISSION -THE ESSENTIAL GUIDE FOR HOME OWNERS
Kenneth A Dijksman. BA(Hons) DipTP, MRTPI   2nd Edition

"For homeowners who want to make alterations to their property but know little or nothing about planning. A jargon free guide written by a professional planner to help you save time and money and make the most of your existing home.

1992   123 pages   ISBN 0 9520553 0 9   £11.95 p&p inc

LIVING WITH A LISTED BUILDING
Josephine M Cormier. ARIBA

Owning a listed building is both a privilege and burden. This book has been written to encourage owners to understand and enjoy their Listed Building and to help them overcome some of the problems and misunderstandings which they may come across in dealing with the law and keeping their buildings in good repair.

1995   90 pages   ISBN 0 9520553 1 7   £14.95 p&p inc

✂ — ✂

PLEASE SEND ME :

No. of
copies:

☐ "LIVING WITH A LISTED BUILDING"
   ISBN 0 9520553 1 7

☐ "PLANNING PERMISSION - THE ESSENTIAL
   GUIDE FOR HOME OWNERS"
   ISBN 0 9520553 0 9

☐ I enclose a cheque for £   p & p inc.

☐ Please invoice me/my company/institution.

☐ Please debit my VISA/ACCESS/MASTERCARD
   CARD NUMBER

Expiry Date _____

NAME : Mr/Mrs/Ms/Miss _____

ADDRESS : _____

_____

POSTCODE :_____   TEL No : _____

SIGNATURE :_____   DATE : _____

We endeavour to despatch all orders within 14 days of receipt. In the event a title is not available, we will record your order and despatch as soon as possible.

If this product fails to satisfy you for whatever reason, we guarantee to refund your money in full, provided the book is returned within 15 days after receipt.

Please return to :

COURTLAND BOOKS
28 Wytham Street,
Oxford,
OX1 4TS

ORDER DIRECT:
(01865) 244168